FASCINATING GOLF STORIES, AND MORE HILARIOUS ADULT GOLF JOKES

Another Golfwell Treasury of the Absolute Best in Golf Stories, and Golf Jokes

Second in the Series of the Bestselling *"Absolutely Hilarious Adult Golf Joke Book"*

Presented by The Team at Golfwell

Published by: Pacific Trust Holdings NZ Ltd., 2016

Golfwell's Fascinating Golf Stories and More Hilarious Adult Golf Jokes

"This book will chase your blues away and put you in a great mood! Just as funny (if not more hilarious than) its predecessor, *"Absolutely Hilarious Adult Golf Joke Book."* Very funny, original, lots of laughs and filled with side-splitting and heartwarming stories. Enjoyed it!"

    -A. Frankton, Denver

"Great stories, especially the lead off story about Arnold Palmer playing his own Bay Hill GC with Tiger Woods with comments from Jack Nicklaus and Bill Murray. Lots of thought provoking quotes, original jokes, and a very fun read. Very good."

    -J. Ferguson, Atlanta

"Excellent with a lot of laughs. Hard to put down. Has a big variety of intelligent stories, R rated jokes, and thinker quotes – all good positive stuff. LOVE IT! great gift to any golfer. Keep them coming, Golfwell Team!"

    -G. Carter, Chicago

Golfwell's Fascinating Golf Stories and More Hilarious Adult Golf Jokes

ADULT CONTENT: This book contains Adult content and is intended for Adults.

FASCINATING GOLF STORIES, AND MORE HILARIOUS ADULT GOLF JOKES Copyright © 2016, Pacific Trust Holdings NZ Ltd. All rights reserved. No part of this book may be reproduced or transmitted in any form or by any means, electronic or mechanical, including photocopying, recording or by any information storage and retrieval system, without written permission from the author, except for brief quotations as would be used in a review.

This book is dedicated to those times when life gets too complicated and a good story or a good laugh solves it all.

Golfwell's Fascinating Golf Stories and More Hilarious Adult Golf Jokes

Contents

1. CELEBRITY GOLF STORIES AND JOKES 9

2. GOLF STORIES – About Dads...............32

3. LAUGH OFF A BAD SHOT - Ever Feel Stupid – I Mean Really Stupid? 36

4. MORE GOLF JOKES AND QUOTES....42

5. OLDER GOLFER JOKES.......................65

6. GOLF STORY: Cape Kidnappers...........81

7. GREAT STORIES AND LONG JOKES FOR THE CLUBHOUSE BAR.....................85

8. MORE JOKES FOR THE CLUBHOUSE BAR (The Wrong Assumption) ... .111

9. LYDIA KO (Growing Up Near Auckland) 119

10. GOLF – FISH STORIES 124

11. AND THE MORAL OF THE STORY IS…(More jokes for the clubhouse bar) ...130

12. GOLFER NICKNAMES…And the Reasons for Them........................145

13. BIG DICK GOLF JOKES 148

14. JOKES FOR DELAYS ON THE COURSE, BACKUPS ON THE TEE OR ANYTIME (Keep a Good Mindset Going) 165

15. A GOLF STORY – Senior Ladies (We love them!) but they can be troublesome… 171

16. ABSOLUTELY HILARIOUS GOLF JOKES 175

17. KEEP LAUGHING 209

"The most wasted of all days is the one without laughter."

- e. e. cummings

"*I always knew what was most important to me. When I was growing up, nothing was more important than golf, but that's the attitude of a young person who hasn't a care in the world. Later on I figured it out. Family was first. Always. Then golf and business come after.*"

    -Arnold Palmer, *A Life Well Played: My Stories*

1. CELEBRITY GOLF STORIES AND JOKES

"How can I intimidate Tiger Woods? I mean, the guy's got 75 or whatever PGA Tour wins, 14 majors. He's been the biggest thing ever in our sport. How could some little 23-year-old from Northern Ireland with a few wins come up and intimidate him."

-Rory McIlroy

Jack Nicklaus wrote an article on how Arnold Palmer was by nature a person who wouldn't give up. When Jack found out about his good friend's death, he said he talked to Arnie about two weeks before his death and Arnie was in Pittsburg looking to get himself better as Arnie wasn't the kind of person to give up.

In 1997, Orlando, Florida. A young Tiger Woods was playing a golf round with Arnold Palmer at the Bay Hill Club and Lodge just a week before Tiger won his first Masters in 1997.

In an excerpt from Arnie's memoir, "A Life Well Played," Arnie describes playing against Tiger who was only 21-years-old at that time. They played and exciting match up to the par 3 very difficult 17th hole.

"We had a friendly little match for $100, and hard as I tried, I couldn't quite hold off a player of that caliber in his prime -- not even on my own golf course.

"Tiger closed me out on the 17th hole. On the 18th tee, deciding that I didn't want to let Tiger get into my pocket without a final effort, I pressed him and challenged Tiger to a one-hole playoff, double or nothing.

"We both hit good drives in the fairway on what is Bay Hill's tough closing par 4 that measures 458 yards and features an oblong green that wraps around a lake. Of course, Tiger was miles ahead of me. I needed a driver to reach the green with my second shot, and I wasn't going to back down. I pulled out the driver. You know: go for broke."

They halved the hole. Tiger was amazed at Arnie's determination never giving up on any of the holes they played and said, "Arnold never gives up…."

Palmer later wrote, "I like to claim, with a wink, that I helped Tiger warm up for his first major championship win."

Bill Murray told a story after Arnie passed on about playing golf with Arnie before the US Senior Open and he was surprised to see Arnie sign autographs and talk with people for 3 hours after their match.

One of our team, Bruce, briefly met Arnie at the bar at Arnie's Bay Hill Club:

"Arnie walked right into the bar. My client and I were staying at Bay Hill and we had one drink with him. We had lots of questions, but Arnie right away turned it around and got us telling him about our boring lives – which he took a sincere interest in. Absolutely an amazing man!"

"Golf is a compromise between what your ego wants you to do, what experience tells you what to do, and what your nerves let you do."

-Bruce Crampton

God and Arnold Palmer are playing golf in heaven and God lets Arnold have the honors on the first tee. There is a huge lake on the left side of the fairway. Arnold tee's off and sends it straight down the middle about 290 yards long leaving a short iron to the green.

"Not too bad." God says.

God steps up and hits its big – almost out of sight but God's ball start to draw too far to the left and splashed into a deep lake.

God walks across the water and waves his hand and the golf ball pops out of the ocean and the Good Lord smacks it with a 3 iron just as it pops out of the ocean and knocks it a foot from the pin.

Arnie says, "Lord, God! Who do you think you are, Tiger Woods?

"He [Donald Trump] is a tough boss. I've known him for decades. He hasn't changed very much. He's a driven person, highly intelligent, and he's very motivated, very charismatic, and he is tough as nails in the sense there's no slack there. You can't put anything over on Donald. Donald can see right through someone trying to dissemble or spin stuff."

-Geraldo Rivera

Obama invited Trump to play golf with two of Obama's regular golf friends.

One of his friends asks him, "Does Trump really has a 5 handicap?"

"He's very good," Obama replies.

Trump is waiting for them at the first tee and after introductions to the two friends of Obama, Trump begins and slices his first tee shot into deep foliage and the ball goes right into the middle of thick bushes.

One friend of Obama's whispers, "You said he was a good golfer!"

Obama says, "Just watch him play."

Trump stands near the thick clump of bushes determining the distance to the green. He grabs a club from his bag and walks through deep foliage and then goes directly into the bushes carrying an iron.

They watch in amazement as his body separates the heavy foliage. They see the iron raise out of the top of the bushes, then hear the swish of a mighty swing. Then the sound of the cracking of small branches, the tearing of leaves, and finally a sharp click as the ball is struck.

One of them points to the green and there is his ball rolling on to the front of the green and stops within four feet of the pin. Trump makes an easy birdie.

On the second hole, a par-3, The Donald hits the ball into the middle of the lake.

The two friends look at Obama again and say "A five handicap? Really? You said he was good."

Obama replies, "Just watch, he's a great player."

Donald walks right into the lake after his ball. Three minutes pass and there's no sign of him. Suddenly they see a hand come out of the water. One of Obama's friends shouts out, "You better dive into the lake to save him, because he's drowning!"

Obama replies "No... that just means he wants a 5 iron."

"Owning a great golf course gives you great power."

-Donald Trump

David Feherty tells a story which happened many years ago about a young assistant club pro, was playing in a tournament in North Ireland. On the final day, he was tied for lead going into the last hole.

Then severe and heavy winds started and some rain began to fall but there wasn't any threat of lightning and it wasn't raining hard enough for the officials to suspend play.

The young pro hit his drive into deep rough and after studying his lie, he chopped his ball out with a wedge but the ball ricocheted off a tree trunk and went out of bounds.

He had to drop another ball. At that time, the rules required the player to drop his ball over his shoulder, but when he turned around he couldn't find it in the heavy wet rough. After searching for it for 5 minutes, he couldn't find it so he had to drop another at the cost of 2 more shots.

After dropping the second ball he played it out. The rain had stopped when he reached the green so he took off his rain jacket and a ball fell out of his hood.

> *"Drinking, it's all shits and giggles until you start to giggle and shit."*
>
> -Anonymous

David Feherty over his career had to deal with his own alcoholism and depression which he made known to the public years ago.

Golf Magazine interviewed him about his issues and he admitted using alcohol "to mask my inner demons".

Tom Cruise had gone public that physical exercise was an excellent way to cure depression or alcohol or drug problems. Feherty, in his unique comic voice said the only the way he could criticize Tom Cruise's suggestion and challenge Tom's thinking were by saying, "...Some sort of exercise would have helped me. Let's say I kicked the shit out of Tom Cruise, that'd be fun and I'd feel a lot better about myself."

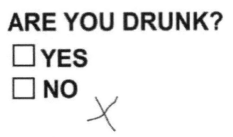

John Daly decided to stop drinking. "I'm going on the wagon, joining AA and no more brew for me, yes sir, I am done. Going to lead a clean life. I want to know what it feels like to wake up without headache."

At the next tournament, John was missing two foot putts, shanking iron shots, whiffing and topping the ball. John's beautiful partner, Anna, was caddying and couldn't believe it. "John, you sure you want to quit drinking?"

"Yes, I do Anna. I have to confess, I am an alcoholic."

"Oh?" the beautiful Anna replied.

"Yes, it's hard to believe but it's true. Even my doctor told me he was surprised to find blood in my alcohol stream and I just got sick and tired of the back of my head getting hit by the toilet seat. Even mosquitoes fell dead off my arms after biting me. But what really did it – I got tired of waking up fully clothed in the bedroom while my underwear wounds up in the bathroom – I can't figure that out."

"My father used to say that it's never too late to do anything you wanted to do. And he said, 'You never know what you can accomplish....'"

- Michael Jordan

At the US Open in June, 2016, Jason Day described his three-year-old son, Dash, as tied for first in the rankings of "The cutest kid in sports." He went on to talk about Dash's preparation for a recent commercial he and his son did:

"He had headphones on and Ellie was helping him out with his lines. I mean, the lines, he's only three, so — and people forget he's three. He's a humongous toddler. He's very big. And you should see Lucy, she's even bigger. She's a fatty. It's fine. Like Ellie, I think she has protein shakes in those things. I don't know what she's doing. But for some reason, she's a very, very big baby. I don't know how other people have real tiny babies."

"Golf is a game of coordination, rhythm and grace; women have these to a great degree."

-Babe Didrickson Zaharias

Tiger Woods was finishing a beer at the private player bar at a Tournament after playing the second round. Tiger made the cut, but another young player who just got his card was paired with him that day missed the cut. The young player came in and sat down next to him.

"Tiger, you've achieved some amazing things in your career. I'll buy you the next round, if you would briefly share some of the wisdom you've learned over the years."

"What do you want to know?" Tiger replied.

I don't know much about women! You've got a lot of experience with women. What do you think of the women you've met in the world?"

Tiger smiled and nodded to the bartender for another beer then began this story:

"I don't know *that* much about women but I do know their age is important.

"Between 18 and 22, a woman is like Africa. Half discovered, half wild, fertile and naturally Beautiful!

"Between 23 and 30, a woman is like Europe. Well-developed and open to trade, especially for someone of real value.

"Between 31 and 35, a woman is like Spain. Very hot, relaxed and convinced of her own beauty.

"Between 36 and 40, a woman is like Greece. Gently aging but still a warm and desirable place to visit.

"Between 41 and 50, a woman is like Great Britain, with a glorious and all conquering past.

"Between 51 and 60, a woman is like Israel. Has been through war, doesn't make the same mistakes twice, takes care of business.

"Between 61 and 70, a woman is like Canada. Self-preserving, but open to meeting new people.

"After 70, she becomes Tibet. Wildly beautiful, with a mysterious past and the wisdom of the ages. An adventurous spirit and a thirst for spiritual knowledge."

The young player said, "That's a fantastic description! You are a very worldly and wise man. Thank you, Tiger."

The young golfer began to leave but before he went out the door, he turned to Tiger and asked one more question.

"Tiger, what about us men? What's the geography of a man?"

"Between the ages of 1 and 90, a man is like North Korea and Zimbabwe; we're simply ruled by a pair of nuts."

"I think these pipe-smokers oughta just move to the next level and go ahead and suck a dick. There's nothing wrong with suckin' dicks. Men do it, women do it; can't be all bad if everybody's doin' it. I say, drop the pipe, and go to the dick! That's my advice. I'm here to help."

— George Carlin, *Brain Droppings*

Rory McIlroy has just taken out a new girl and drove her back to her home after being out together. When they reach the front door he leans with one hand on the wall and says to her, "Sweetie, why don't you give me a blowjob?"

"What? You're crazy!" she said.

"Look, don't worry," he said. "It will be quick, I promise you."

"Noooo! Someone may see us, a neighbor, anybody..."

"At this time of the night no one will show up. C'mon, sweetie, I really need it."

"I've already said NO, and NO is final!"

"Honey, it'll just be a really small blowie... I know you like it too."

"NO!!! I've said NO!!!"

Desperately, Rory says, "My love, don't be like that. I promise you I love you and I really need this blowjob."

At this moment, the older sister shows up at the door in her nightgown and half asleep.

Rubbing her eyes, she says: "Dad says, 'Dammit, give him the blowjob or I'll have to blow him. But for God's sake, tell your boyfriend to take his hand off the intercom button so the rest of the family can get some sleep.'"

"I don't think I've ever stepped into a gym – they won't let me smoke there. I just thank God Miller Lite is not as fattening as most beers. If I cut back on beer, though, I'd look anorexic."

-John Daly

The club blowhard was mouthing off on the 19th hole. "Some very famous celebrities play golf. For example, O.J. Simpson, Ted Kennedy, and President Bill Clinton are all golfers?"

"Yes? Well so what? Lots of famous people play golf?" said a guy at the bar.

The bartender hears this and adds, "We all know O.J.'s a slicer, Ted Kennedy can't drive over water, and Clinton hits a lot of holes but can't seem to hit the right hole!"

"Just because a man lacks the use of his eyes doesn't mean he lacks vision."

-Stevie Wonder

Stevie Wonder and Jack Nicklaus are in a bar. Nicklaus asks Stevie, "How is the singing career going?"

Stevie says, "Okay. The latest album is in the top 10, so it's pretty good. How's the golf?"

"Not bad, I'm not competing but have other things going on. My swing isn't what it used to be."

Stevie says, "When my swing goes wrong I need to stop playing for a while and think about it, then the next time I play it's better."

"You play golf!?" asks Jack.

Stevie says, "Yeah, I have been playing for years."

"You're still blind, aren't you? How can you play golf if you're blind?" Jack asks.

"I get my caddie to stand in the middle of the fairway and he yells out to me. I listen for the sound of his voice and play the ball towards him. Then when I get to where the ball lands my caddie moves to the green or further down the fairway and again I play the ball towards his voice," explains Stevie.

"But how the heck do you putt?" Nicklaus asked.

"Well, I get my caddie to lean down in front of the hole and call to me with his head on the ground and I just play the ball to the sound and distance of his voice."

Nicklaus says, "Okay, okay. What's your handicap?"

"Well, I'm a plus 2 right now," Stevie says.

Nicklaus is amazed and asks Stevie, "We must play a game sometime."

Stevie says, "Well, people don't take me seriously so I only play for money, and I never play for less than $50,000 a hole."

Nicklaus thinks it over and says, "Okay, let's do it. When would you like to play?"

"Oh, any night next week is fine with me."

"That's another thing about my father. He made me very conscious of the fact I wasn't very good and I had to prove to him that I was good. And that hung with me, and I always wanted to play golf with him and show him. He said 'Never, Never tell anyone how good you are. Show them!'

-Arnold Palmer

2. GOLF STORIES – About Dads

Arnold Palmer's father, Deacon Palmer, starting working on the grounds crew at the LaTrobe Country Club and eventually got to play well enough to get a job giving golf lesson. He worked both as being in charge of the grounds crew and as the teaching pro.

Deacon didn't give Arnold lessons. Instead he encouraged Arnold to use trial and error and let his son learn on his own, except he encouraged Arnold to hit the ball hard.

Arnold use to say he could never hit the ball hard enough to suit his father.

Jack Nicklaus's father, Charlie Nicklaus, saw his son Jack start to play golf at an early age and Jack couldn't get enough of it. His father would bring Jack along to the Scioto Country Club where Jack use to love to hit balls on the range. He didn't tell his father how many buckets he would go through but where the average golfer used on or perhaps two buckets, Jack's dad would get a bill for 10 to 11 buckets that Jack went through each day on the range.

Tom Watson's father, Ray Watson, was a very good golfer and one year made the quarter finals of the US Amateur. Tom and his dad competed against each other at the Walloon Lake Country Club for the club championship when Tom was 14 years old. Tom was ahead by two with three holes to play. When they walked off the 18th, Ray had squared the match. On the first playoff hole, Ray had over a 20-footer for par and Tom had a 15-footer for birdie. Ray made the putt, but Tom didn't. On the second playoff hole, Tom had a three-foot putt to stay alive but his father wouldn't concede it and Tom missed it and lost the club championship. Tom reflected on this match and said he learned there and then that no one gives you anything in life. The next year Tom beat his dad for the club championship.

Phil Mickelson dad, Phil Sr., finally gave in to Phil begging to go with his dad to play golf at the Balboa Park Country Club, but his dad didn't think the club would allow a three-year-old on the course. Phil persisted in begging his dad to play and Phil Sr. got his son to play with him. Phil loved it and moved along the course well except when they came to the 18th hole which Phil didn't want to play since it was the final hole and that meant he couldn't play anymore.

3. LAUGH OFF A BAD SHOT - Ever Feel Stupid – I Mean Really Stupid?

"Only two things are infinite, the universe and human stupidity, and I'm not sure about the former."

    -Albert Einstein

Feeling stupid (who hasn't?) Embarrassment from a stupid golf shot tends to make the next shot even more difficult since your muscles are now tensed from the embarrassment. The following stories are true. Remember these after making a bad shot and enjoy a laugh.

A man on San Jose, used his shotgun like a club to break his ex's car windshield. The gun discharged when he did it and he blew a hole in his gut.

Los Angeles police were having 5 men in a line up to catch a robbery suspect when one of them just had to correct the detectives when they asked each one of them to repeat the words, "Give me your money or I'll shoot." He had to tell them, "That's not what I said."

A mechanic in Alamo Michigan trying to repair a truck, asked a friend to drive the truck at a high speed while he hung on underneath so he could see what was causing an unknown noise. Despite several "Don't do its" he got his clothes caught and his friend found the mechanic wrapped around the driveshaft.

An Ohio man walked into a police station with a wire sticking out of his forehead claiming someone had stolen his brain and he wanted to be x-rayed to prove it. He had apparently drilled a hole in his head looking for his brain and put wire in to search for his brain.

A Detroit man watched on as police were showing school children their new car computer which located felons. The Detroit man stepped up and asked more about how it worked. The police asked him for his license and ran it through the computed and then arrested him for being wanted for an armed robbery in St. Louis two years earlier.

A North Carolina man awoke in the early morning by his bedside telephone ringing loudly. He inadvertently grabbed his handgun which he kept on his nightstand thinking it was his phone and the gun discharged when he put it to his head killing him.

A man in England received a notice in the mail that he was caught by a police camera speeding in his car and received a 40-pound fine along with a photo of his car. Instead of paying the fine, the man sent the police a photo of a 40-pound note. Police then sent the man a photo of handcuff. The man paid the fine.

A South Carolina prison inmate on a murder conviction spent several years waiting for his appeals on his not going to the electric chair. The appellate courts reduced his sentence to life in prison but while he was sitting on a metal toilet in his cell trying to fix a TV, he bit into a wire and electrocuted himself.

A New Jersey couple were injured when a one-quarter stick of dynamite blew up in their car at 2am. They were driving a long time and being bored they lit the dynamite "to see what would happen" and tried to toss it out the window at 2am and told police they didn't notice the car windows were closed.

An Indiana man used a gas lighter to look down and check the barrel of a musket rifle that hadn't been firing well and was killed when the weapon discharged in his face when he ignited the powder of the loaded musket.

Two young Canadian men both died in a head on crash while playing a game of "Chicken" on their snowmobiles which resulted in a tie game.

Another Canadian man fell to his death while he was cleaning his bird feeder on the balcony of his apartment on the 23rd floor. He had to stand on something to reach up to the birdfeeder and chose another's wheelchair to stand on which moved while he was cleaning and he went over the balcony.

A Michigan defendant was on trial for Drug Possession and he raised the defense of being searched without a warrant. The prosecutor argued that the officers had reasonable cause to search him since there was a bulge in his jacket which could have been a firearm. The defendant disagreed and testified he was actually wearing the same jacket in court and took off his jacket and handed it to the judge to show him. The judge discovered a packet of cocaine in the jacket and the judge began laughing so hard he had to call a five-minute recess.

Two Arkansas men were severely injured when their pickup truck went off the road and hit a tree a little after midnight. They were returning at night from a long trip catching frogs. The headlights on the truck were not working properly since the headlight fuse had burned out. They didn't have a spare fuse but one of the men found that his 22-caliber bullet would fit perfectly in the fuse box of the old pickup truck and got the headlights working. But after going for a half an hour or so, the bullet discharged and struck one of the men in the balls. That's when the pickup left the road and struck the tree. The highway trooper was amazed the men admitted how this occurred. When the wife of the man who was shot in the balls was informed of the accident, she inquired how many frogs did they get and if anyone had bothered to get the frogs out of the truck.

4. MORE GOLF JOKES AND QUOTES

Romance on the Driving Range

John played golf every Wednesday with his usual group. He and the rest of his foursome admired a voluptuous single woman who practiced on the driving range at the same time John's group teed off. John lusted for her but he was nervous and couldn't figure out how to meet her. He was too polite to approach her on the range and interrupt her practicing. He looked around the club for her every time he was at the club. He asked about her, but no one seemed to know who she was. John was determined to meet her and spent sleepless nights thinking how he could approach her.

One night he had a dream. In the dream, he was hitting balls on the practice range but this time he pulled out of his golf bag a bright fluorescent orange driver, brighter in color than any driver he'd ever seen. It looked magnificent. John was hitting the orange driver farther than he'd ever hit a golf ball in his life. While he was hitting balls out of sight with it, the beautiful woman approached him.

"Excuse me." She said. "I couldn't help but notice the orange driver you are using. You are hitting it very well!"

"Oh, here try it yourself, you'll be amazed in the difference in distance." John said, then handed her the driver and she smiled and gave it a try. Sure enough, the gorgeous woman hit balls even further than John. They began to talk and John introduced himself.

"My name is John. I've seen you here practicing every Wednesday and wanted to meet you. But no one here at the club seems to know you?"

"Oh, my name is Vanessa." Her sweet sexy voice made John yearn with desire. Vanessa continued talking to John in the dream, and John focused on her beautiful red lips as she mouthed her words in seemingly slow motion:

"I'm cursed with being so attractive. Men keep bothering me -- interrupting me. I try to keep to myself, it's better that way. The attention I get is sooo annoying." She said.

"Aaah, you have my sympathy, you poor woman! I understand how you feel. You certainly are very attractive. Here, why don't you try out this driver more and I'll hit over there. Just give it back to me when you're finished. And, I'll stand here so no one will bother you."

"Why thank you! You are very nice." John smiled and after the beautiful woman finished hitting John's driver they began to talk and got along so well, John politely asked her out for dinner and she happily accepted.

"Briiinggg!" John's alarm goes off and he wakes up and jumps out of bed and he didn't waste any time getting his driver. He carefully painted the head on his driver a bright fluorescent orange and rushed out with the orange driver early to the range and began to hit balls just as the gorgeous young woman was walking up to hit balls on the range. She noticed the orange driver and went up to talk to him.

"Excuse me." She said in a very sweet voice. "I couldn't help but notice the orange driver you are using. You are hitting it very well!"

"Yes." John said. "This orange driver is magic! Do you want to fuck?"

British Comedian Nick Frost: "I also like golf but don't get to play much. My golf tip? Don't f*cking bother. Most annoying game ever, but it has me now. I've got a handicap of 26, which is terrible but I enjoy it.

Simon Pegg: "I live next to a golf course now so I'm absolutely determined to play."

Nick Frost: "You'll be tearing your hair out."

Simon Pegg: "But I want to get into the zone of it and not be angered by it. Just be like "Yeah, whatevs", even if I miss."

Simon Pegg (later): "I do get very angry at things. My wife has to count to ten because if she gets annoyed at me being annoyed, then I get annoyed at her being annoyed at me being annoyed."

-Excerpt from Pegg and Frost's world of fitness, The Shortlist.

Simon forgot his wedding anniversary and his wife was ticked off at him.

She told him, "Tomorrow morning, I expect to find a gift in the driveway that goes from 0 to 200 in under 6 seconds, AND IT BETTER BE THERE."

The next morning, Simon got up really early.

When his wife woke up a couple of hours later, she looked out the window, and sure enough, there was a small gift-wrapped box sitting in the middle of the driveway.

Confused, the wife put on her robe, ran out to the driveway, and took the box into the house.

She opened it, and found a brand-new bathroom scale.

Simon is not yet well enough to have visitors.

"Having played golf for years, I took all the lessons, read all the books, watched the pros play, got the latest in equipment and it just drives me insane on why I haven't improved. Sometimes, I stand quietly on the green watching the other golfers and wonder why I'm not in a mental institution. Then I realize…maybe I already am?"

- Anonymous

A psychiatrist was doing his morning rounds at a mental hospital when he entered a patient's room.

He found Patient #1 sitting on the floor, pretending to sink a putt but he didn't have a putter or golf ball. Patient #2 was hanging from the ceiling, by his feet.

The doctor asked patient #1 what he was doing. The patient replied, "Can't you see I'm trying to sink this putt?"

The doctor asked Patient #1 what Patient #2 was doing.

Patient #1 replied, "Oh. He's my friend, but he's a little crazy. He thinks he's a light bulb."

The doctor looked up and noticed that the Patient hanging from the ceiling face was getting very red.

The doctor asks Patient #1, "If he's your friend, don't you think you should get him down from there before he hurts himself."

Patient #1 replies, "What? How can I putt in the dark?"

"The Supreme Court ruled that disabled golfer Casey Martin has a legal right to ride in a golf cart between shots at PGA Tour events. Man, the next thing you know, they're going to have some guy carry his clubs around for him."

- Jon Stewart

There once was a farmer whose wife had died and left him with three beautiful teenage daughters.

They lived next to a golf course and many young men who played the course noticed the daughters and many young men sought eagerly to date them.

All the young men had heard the beautiful teenage daughters went out on dates with different young men every Saturday. They had their pick of suitors and were choosy but loved it.

But, the farmer would stand at the door with his shotgun, making it clear to their suitors he wanted no shenanigans from them.

Another Saturday night came around. About 7 p.m., there was a knock on the door. The farmer answered the door with shotgun in hand. The young golfer said,

"Hi, my name's Joe. I'm here for Flo. I'm taking her to the show. Is she ready to go?"

The farmer thought Joe was very cool and told them to enjoy themselves.

A few minutes later, another knock was heard. A second golfer appeared and said,

"Hi, I'm Eddie. I'm here for Betty. I'm taking her for spaghetti. I hope she's ready."

The farmer laughed and thought Eddie was very cool and told them to enjoy themselves.

A few minutes after that, a third knock was heard.

"Hi, I'm Chuck..." The farmer shot him.

"You could put a blond wig on a hot-water heater and some dude would try to fuck it."

-Tina Fey, from "Bossypants"

A young blonde woman is distraught because she fears her husband is having an affair. He tells her he's just out playing golf, but he leaves his golf clubs in the garage, so she goes to a gun shop and buys a hunting rifle.

A few days later, she comes home to find her husband in bed having sex with a beautiful brunette.

She grabs the gun and holds it to her own head.

The husband stops his lovemaking and gets out of the bed and begs her, "HONEY! Don't shoot yourself! It's not worth it baby! I don't love this woman! I love you!"

Filled with anger, the blonde responds to the husband, "Shut up...you're next!"

"Golf without bunkers and hazards would be tame and monotonous. So would life."

-B. C. Forbes

One day, Heaven finally became very full, and something had to be done. The Lord decided to have St. Peter check everyone at the gate and ask each one how they died. If it was a grisly story where the good person died a horrible death, they would be allowed into Heaven. But if not, they had to wait in Purgatory, or even Hell, until there was room in heaven for them.

A large line formed at the gates of heaven. The first man tells Peter this story:

"Well, for a while I'd been suspecting my wife of cheating on me. So, today instead of playing 18 holes of golf, I only played nine and came home early to see if I could catch her. Sure enough, I got to my apartment and she was lying naked on the bed.

I looked all over the apartment searching for the guy but couldn't find him. Then I remembered that we lived on the 25th floor of an apartment building, and there's a balcony. So, I rushed out to the balcony and there he was hanging off holding the railing.

I beat at his hands with my nine iron and he just wouldn't let go, so I ran and got my driver and beat his hands more until he fell into the bushes below.

I saw the bastard was still alive so I wheeled out the refrigerator and pushed it over the balcony on top of him. But the strain of the effort gave me a heart attack and I died!

"Wow!" St. Peter said. "That really is bad! You can go ahead...you poor guy!"

The next man told St. Peter this story:

"I live on the 26th floor of an apartment building, and every day I do exercises on my balcony but I exercised too hard fell over the edge. I had the presence of mind to catch the railing of the balcony below me.

Suddenly, this guy comes running out and started beating at my hands with a golf club. He ran back inside and I thought I was safe, but then he came back out with another golf club and beat my hands again until I finally fell off. I landed in the bushes below and they broke my fall and saved my life.

But that wasn't enough for this guy! He sees me lying in the bushes then disappears inside then I see this refrigerator coming down at me and the guy is laughing his head off! The refrigerator squashed me flat and killed me. And now I'm here."

"Wow, that's a good one too! You can go ahead..." St. Peter said.

The third man in line told St. Peter this story:

"I don't know what happened. I was hiding naked inside this refrigerator..."

Jessica Simpson from the "Newlyweds" show:

"Is this chicken, what I have, or is this fish? I know it's tuna, but it says 'Chicken… by the Sea.'"

For the clubhouse bar:

One day a brunette, a redhead and a blonde decide to go through their daughter's purses.

So, the brunette goes through her daughter's purse and finds cigarettes.

She says, "Oh my god, I'm so ashamed! My Daughter smokes."

So, the redhead goes through her daughter's purse and finds an empty can of beer.

She says, "Oh my god I'm so ashamed! My daughter drinks."

So, finally, it's the blondes turn and she finds a used condom. She says, "Oh my god I'm so ashamed! My daughter has a penis!"

"If we knew what we were doing, it would not be called research, would it?"

-Albert Einstein

Four New Zealand golfers were delayed during a round watching a very slow Australian foursome in front of them.

One of them remarked, "Those Ozzy guys are wankers. Slowest I've ever seen."

Trying to lighten things up, another Kiwi golfer told a story:

"Did you guys know scientists in Britain did a study to determine why the head on a man's' penis is larger than the shaft.

"The study took two years and cost over $1.2 million. The finding was the head was larger than the shaft to give the man more pleasure.

"After the results were published, France decided to conduct their own study on the same subject as the French, of course, know more about sex than the Brits. After four years of intensive research at a cost of more than $4 million, the French researchers finally concluded the head of a man's penis is larger than the shaft to provide the woman with more pleasure during sex.

"When the results of the French study were released, Australias decided to conduct their own study. The Aussies didn't really trust the British or French studies. So, after nearly 5 minutes of intensive research and a cost of $75.00 (48 beers), the Aussies completed their study.

"The Aussies found the reason the head on a man's penis is larger is to prevent your hand from flying off and hitting you in the nose.

"Women fake orgasms to have relationships. Men fake relationships to have orgasms."

-Anonymous

A golfer trying to make his tee time was totally focused on getting through heavy traffic on the expressway.

He changed lanes every minute trying to inch ahead. Finally, he gets clear of the traffic but carefully stops at a stop sign, as he didn't want to get stopped for rolling a stop sign, and glances up at his rear-view mirror and sees a huge SUV barreling at him at high speed. He's rear ended only two blocks from the course. A beautiful young lady crawls out of her demolished SUV and amazingly, neither of them were hurt.

She says to him, "So you're a man, that's interesting. And I'm a woman." She paused and looked back at the cars, "Wow! Just look at our cars. There's nothing left, but fortunately we are unhurt. This must be a sign from God that we should meet and become friends and live together in peace the rest of our days."

The golfer, still staggering around half dazed, replied, "I agree with you completely; this must be a sign from God!"

The woman continued. "And look at this - here's another miracle. My car is completely demolished but this half gallon bottle of red wine didn't break. Surely God wants us to drink this wine and celebrate our good fortune."

So, she hands the bottle to the man. The golfer still dazed nods his head in agreement, opens it and takes a few big swigs from the bottle, then hands it back to the woman.

The woman takes the bottle, immediately puts the cap back on, and hands it back to the golfer.

He takes the bottle and asks, "Aren't you having any?"

The woman replies, "No. I think I will just wait for the police..."

"All you can do is really the prep work and make sure you're ready to hit each golf shot. Outside of that, you're not sure really what's going to happen. It's a funny game, but I think that's why I love it. You never know, one day to the next; you could go shoot 62, and the next day you're going to shoot 78, and you can't predict it."

- Rickie Fowler

A golfer dials home from the golf course. A strange woman answers. The golfer says, "Who is this?"

"This is the maid." answered the woman.

"We don't have a maid!"

"I was just hired this morning by the lady of the house."

"Well, this is her husband. Is she there?"

"Ummm...she's upstairs in the bedroom with someone who I just figured was her husband."

The guy is fuming. He thinks back on how his wife was in such a rush to get him out of the house this morning and says to the maid, "Listen, would you like to make $50,000?"

"Sure, what do I have to do?"

"Get the shotgun out of the hall closet, go upstairs and shoot that unfaithful witch and the jerk she's with."

The maid puts down the phone. The guy hears footsteps, followed by a couple of shotgun blasts.

The maid comes back to the phone. "What should I do with the bodies?"

"Throw them in the swimming pool!"

"What pool?"

"Uh...is this 555-2277?"

5. OLDER GOLFER JOKES

"Let us never know what old age is. Let us know the happiness time brings, and not count the years."

   -Ausonius

A Question Survey on the difficulties of growing older was given to senior pro golfers who were all members of the Champions Tour over the age of 70 and well thought of by their competitors as being very wise.

These were some of the responses:

Q. Where can men over the age of 70 find younger women who might be interested in them?

A: Try a bookstore, under FICTION or have a few hundreds fall out of your back pocket.

Q: What can a man do during the very difficult times when his wife is having annoying hot flashes and experiencing menopause?

A: Keep busy. If you're handy with tools, you can finish the basement. When you're done, and make sure you build it very comfortably as you will have a place to live.

Q: How do you deal with your wife having that terrible curse of the elderly wrinkles?

A: Take off your glasses.

Q: Seriously! What do you tell your wife to get rid of the crow's feet and all those wrinkles on her face?

A: Go braless. It will usually pull them out.

Q: Why do the 70-plus Champion Tour player use valet parking at golf tournaments?

A: Valets don't forget where they park your car.

Q: Is it common for 70-plus year olds to have problems with short term memory storage?

A: Storing memory is not a problem. Retrieving it is the problem.

Q: As you age, do you find yourself sleeping more soundly?

A: Yes, but usually in the afternoon.

Q: Where should 70-plus year olds players look for their eye glasses?

A: On their foreheads.

Q. What do most of your players say when they visit the interior and see the furnishings in the Clubhouse just off the 18th green at the Old Course in St. Andrews which originated in the early 15th Century?

A. Gee, I remember some of these.

Golfwell's Fascinating Golf Stories and More Hilarious Adult Golf Jokes

A Man reading the side effects warnings on a bottle: 'Dizziness, impotence, anal leakage, memory loss, shaking, shortness of breath, impotence, bleeding from the ears, nose and gums, flatulence, projectile vomiting….'

"Hell, maybe I'll just live with the runny nose for a while?"

-Anonymous

A retired golfer suffered a heart attack on the course and was convalescing in a hospital room on the cardiac floor. The doctor told him he might not be able to have sex again.

Pondering a life where he wouldn't be of much use to his wife anymore, he laid on the bed wearing an oxygen mask over his mouth and nose.

A young nurse came to cleanse his body with sponge.

The patient mumbled, "Are my testicles black?"

Nurse replied, "I don't know Sir, I am just setting up to give you a bath."

The patient repeated, "Are my testicles black?"

Nurse was quite embarrassed to answer the question and said "Sir everything should be all right."

The patient just kept on asking again and again, "Are my testicles black?"

Nurse could not bear a patient concerned so much.

So, she raised his gown, moved her hand to find and grab his penis and testicle, moved it all around, checked very closely and suddenly the man ejaculated on nurse's hand.

The man pulls off his oxygen mask, embarrassed at the fiasco said loudly, "Nurse, thanks very much, but I still need to know, are my tests results back?"

Actor, John Barrymore was in a rush beelining for a bathroom and mistakenly went into the ladies' bathroom and began frantically searching for a urinal. A woman is standing there:

Woman: "How Dare you! This is for ladies!"

*John Barrymore: "And so, madam, is **this**."*

   -John Barrymore

Harold's wife said to him "It's about time that you learned to play golf.

That's the game where you chase a ball all over the countryside when you are too old to chase women."

So, Harold went to see his friend Mike who was a keen golfer and asked him if he could teach him how to play golf.

This is what Harold said Mike told him about golf:

Mike said, "You've got balls, haven't you?"

Harold said "Yes, but sometimes on a cold morning they're kinda hard to find."

"Bring them to the clubhouse tomorrow," he said, "And we'll tee off."

"What's tee off?" Harold asked.

"It's a golf term and we have to tee off in front of the clubhouse."

"Not for me, you can tee off there if you like but I'll tee off behind the barn somewhere."

"No, no, a tee is a little thing about the size of your pinky finger."

"Yeah, I've got one of those!" Harold said.

"Well, you stick it in the ground and put your balls on top of it." Mike said.

"How do play golf sitting down? I always thought you stood up and walked around."

"You do. You are standing when your ball is on the tee."

Well, Harold thought that was stretching a little thing too far, and he said so.

Mike continued. "You got a bag, haven't you?"

"Of course," Harold said.

"Your balls are in it, aren't they?"

"Of course…"

"Well, can't you open your bag and take one out?"

Harold thought, "I suppose I could." But he was damned if he was going to.

"Don't you have a zipper on the bag?" Mike asked.

"No, I am the old-fashioned type."

"Do you know how to hold your club?"

Well after 50 years, Harold thought he should have some sort of idea, and told him so.

Mike said to take his club in both hands.

Harold knew right then he didn't know what Mike was talking about.

Then he said, "You swing it over your shoulders."

Harold said, "That's not me, that's my brother you're talking about."

Mike asked, "How do you hold your club?"

Harold said, "In two fingers."

"That's not right." Mike said, as he got behind Harold, put both arms around him and told him to bend over and he would show him how.

Harold thought "He can't catch me there, because I didn't put in three years in the Navy for nothing."

"You hit the ball with your club and it will soar and soar."

Harold said that he could well imagine.

Then Mike said, "When you are on the green -- "

"What's a green?" said Harold.

"That's where the hole is."

"Sure. You're not color blind?"

"No. Then you take your putter – "

"What's a putter?"

"That's the smallest club made."

That's what I've got - a putter, thought Harold.

With it, you put your ball in the hole.

Harold corrected him, "You mean the putter."

"No, the hole isn't big enough for the ball and the putter."

Well, Harold thought, *I've seen holes big enough for a horse and wagon.*

Then Mike said, "after you make the first hole, you go on to the next seventeen."

He wasn't talking to me, thought Harold. *After two holes, I'm shot to hell.*

"You mean, you can't make eighteen holes in one day?"

"Hell no, I make one hole in eighteen days, besides how do I know I'm in the 18th hole?"

"The flag will go up."

That would be just my luck, thought Harold.

"It is a rare and difficult attainment to grow old gracefully and happily."

-Arnold Palmer

An older man met a younger woman at his golf club and dated her and she agreed to live with him.

Trouble soon developed for the mature guy when he prematurely ejaculated every time the young lady would take her clothes off or if he made it through that, he would come as soon as he penetrated.

He was going to talk to his friends but was too embarrassed so he called his doctor for advice and the doctor told him to masturbate before sex.

The man decided, "Okay, I'll try it."

But, he couldn't figure out where to masturbate before he came home. No way could he do it in his office. The restroom? No, that was too open. He considered out back in an alley, but that was too unsafe.

Finally, on his way home, he pulled his truck over on the side of the highway just before he turned down the street to his house. He got out and crawled underneath, pretending to be fixing something under the truck.

He pulled down his pants and started to jerk off. He couldn't concentrate so he closed his eyes and thought of his young lover slowly taking her clothes off in front of him. As he grew closer to orgasm, he felt someone pulling his pants off.

Not wanting to lose his mental fantasy or the orgasm, he kept his eyes shut and shouted, "WHAT THE HELL?!"

"This is the police. *What the hell* are you doing?"

"I'm checking out the axle, it's busted."

"Well, you better check your brakes because your truck rolled down the hill a few minutes ago."

"You might be on the back nine of life, but it's good to finish strong."

-Morton Shaevitz, Refire! Don't Retire: Make the Rest of Your Life the Best of Your Life

A woman who is constantly embarrassed by her husband falling asleep in church goes to the pastor to ask for help.

The pastor says, "Look luv, if he falls asleep again, poke him with this hat pin. I'll nod to you as a signal to poke him." The woman agrees to the plan.

So, Sunday rolls around and sure enough, good old Mr. Jones nods off again. The pastor notices and asks, "Who is our savior?" then nods to Mrs. Jones.

She pokes her husband, and he wakes up and shouts, "Jesus Christ!".

The pastor, pretending to be impressed, says, "Very good!".

A full three minutes later, Mr. Jones is asleep again. The pastor again notices, and asks, "What is the name of Jesus' father?" before nodding at Mrs. Jones again.

She pokes her husband, who screams, "GOD!" at the top of his lungs.

The pastor again congratulates Mr. Jones on his alertness and continues with the sermon.

However, during the sermon, the pastor begins nodding and moving his head as his sermon gets more intense, which Mrs. Jones mistakes for a poking signal.

The priest then says, "And what did Eve say to Adam after she gave him his 99th child?" the pastor continues his head moving.

The mistaken Mrs. Jones pokes her husband, and he shouts, "If you poke that fucking thing into me one more time, I'll snap it in half and shove it up your ass!"

6. GOLF STORY: Cape Kidnappers

"At the 6th and 15th holes, it's possible to pull your approach off the very end of the earth, though it will take nearly 10 seconds of hang time for your ball to reach the ocean, 500 feet below."

— Tom Doak, Course Designer

The picture shows the 14th, 15th and 16th holes at Kidnappers. Besides these, there are several other holes right on the Pacific Ocean with amazing views.

Cape Kidnappers is a long way from the US and the UK. It's located in Hawkes Bay, New Zealand. The signature hole is the l5th, and named, "Pirate's Plank. " Being 650 yards long, it requires four straight shots to reach the green for most players.

The drama starts on the tee when you think about the 65 foot drop into a cavern along the right side and a 500 foot drop on the left side. We've played

Kidnappers and if you are afraid of heights, this hole is troublesome. If you overshoot the green, there is a 500 foot drop off the back

I hooked my third shot to the left trying to hit it harder and never saw that ball again. Here are a few reviews from others on this fabulous course.:

"Unbelievable"

"I have played some of the best courses in the US and this is right up there. God designed an amazing view and incredible property and Doak did a fantastic job turning it into a World Class Golf Course. Great staff, terrific conditions and views you can't replicate."

"Experience of a Lifetime"

"Incredible course. Breathtaking views. The drive in alone made it worthwhile. Stayed in Napier the night before (unexpected pleasure), and then played the course solo first thing in the morning. Felt like a little piece of heaven."

"Difficult golf course with unmatched cliff beauty"

"If you are reading this review, you know the story of Cape Kidnappers. Something like 8000 acres were bought by Julian Robertson and turned into an amazing but very hard golf course and also a Gannet preservation area to help bring back these native birds."

The small town of Napier is close to this course about 15 minutes away to the front gate. By the way, it takes at least 10-15 minutes to drive from the front gate to the pro shop since there's several thousand acres to drive through.

Hawkes Bay is a wine growing region with world class wineries and fine wines.

But make sure you're somewhat sober playing this course as it's important to watch your step on the tee on the 16th, "Widow's Walk". It's a long way down if you back up too far trying to line up your tee shot.

The 16th tee is also the only place on the entire course you can view the Black Reef lying out in the Pacific Ocean 500 feet below.

7. GREAT STORIES AND LONG JOKES FOR THE CLUBHOUSE BAR

"You may tell a tale that takes up residence in someone's soul and becomes their blood and self and purpose."
(or at least give them a good laugh?)
    -Erin Morgenstern, The Night Circus

After finishing a round at Royal Mougins Golf Club on the French Riviera, an accountant, on his own, walked along the beaches of the Cote d' Azur for the first time. He'd been working very hard and needed a break so he decided to treat himself to an extravagant holiday.

A bit lonely, he sat on his beach towel wearing dark wraparound sunglasses and watched the girls on the beach. He noticed a Frenchman, just about the same age as him walking the beach and being followed by five gorgeous women, all bare breasted, slowly following the man.

The Frenchman walked by the accountant on his way to the refreshment stand and the accountant had to interrupt him. The beautiful women stood by at a distance.

"Monsieur, may I have a word with you?"

"Oui, what eez on your mind?" said the Frenchman.

"Excusez-moi, but I couldn't help but notice the beautiful women following you along the beach. How do you do that?" The accountant asked.

"Monsieur, do you know the secret?"

"What secret?" asked the accountant.

"Well, before you take zee walk on zee beach, you place zee potato in zee swimsuit," said the Frenchman.

"Oooh, I see! Yes, I see," said the accountant.

So, the accountant rushed off to the market and bought a big potato and came back to the beach and walked for hours up and down the beach, but absolutely no women were following him.

He couldn't figure it out! Then he noticed the French guy and jogged up to him.

"Listen, I've got a potato and put it in my swimsuit and I've been walking up and down this beach for hours and no women follow me? They don't even notice me?" said the accountant.

The Frenchman paused and looked the accountant up and down. "Monsieur, you place zee potato in zee *front* of the swimsuit."

To my greedy relatives who are only waiting for me to pass on from this world, I plan my last words to be: "I left you all millions in cash underneath the green on the 18th hole of the golf course called…."

-Anonymous

A Frenchman, an Englishman and a New Yorker were captured by cannibals while playing at a very remote golf course in Papua New Guinea. The cannibals bound them, then dragged them through the jungle for miles.

Finally arriving at the Village, the chief comes to them and says,

"The bad news is we've caught you and we're going to kill you and this is how we are going to do it: We will first slowly peel all of your skin off your bodies. We will put the rest of you in a pot, cook you, and eat you. Then we are going to build a large war canoe. We will stretch your skins to cover the outside of the canoe and make it watertight. The good news is that you can choose how to die."

The Frenchman says, "I take zee sword."

The chief gives him a sword, the Frenchman says, "Vive la France!" and runs himself through.

The Englishman says, "A pistol for me, please."

The chief gives him a pistol, the Englishman points it at his head and says, "God save the Queen!" and blows his brains out.

The New Yorker says, "Gimme a fuckin' fork."

The chief is puzzled. He slowly walks around the New Yorker looking him up and down. The chief shrugs and gives him a fork.

The New Yorker takes the fork and starts jabbing himself all over--the stomach, the sides, the chest, everywhere. There is blood coming out all over, it's horrible.

The chief is appalled and asks, "My God, what are you doing?"

Still poking himself, he says, "Fuck your canoes!"

When my time on this good earth is done,

And all my activities here are passed,

I want them to bury me upside down,

And all my critics, can kiss my ass."

-Bobby Knight

A True Story

My wife and I visited the Natandola Bay Golf Course in Fiji. She went shopping and so I played the course with another single player, an older gentleman. "Call me Bud." He said.

After we teed off the first hole, we drove up the fairway and were lining up our second shots. We heard the sound of another golf cart coming up behind us. It was the assistant pro.

"I just got a single player who'd like to join you." He said.

I looked back and saw a young woman standing on the first tee with her club in hand and a ball teed up.

"Fine!" I quickly said. The assistant pro turned and drove back to the young woman. Then, realizing I hadn't asked Bud if it was fine with him, I glanced at him and he was frowning.

"Hey, I'm sorry, Bud, I didn't ask you first. I just thought – "

Bud interrupted, "I don't like playing with a woman. They aren't good and don't hit very far and she'll slow us down.... but, it's fine...."

We drove off the fairway allowing her to hit. We watched in silent awe as her drive flew over us landing 20 yards ahead.

The attractive young lady drove up smiling and we exchanged introductions.

She was a South Korean and played golf for several years, and was touring Australia, New Zealand, and Fiji with a friend and had an 8 handicap. Bud was disgruntled with it all.

When she made a long 25-foot putt on the third green she walked past Bud and bent over and picked her ball out of the cup, Bud wryly said, "Nice Butt!"

The young lady blushed a bit and didn't say anything. A somber silence followed.

On the next hole, Bud played bad mishitting every ball and eventually picked up on the hole.

On the next tee, I told this joke: "A man comes home from work and finds his wife admiring her breasts in the mirror. He asks, "What are you doing?"

The wife replies, "I went to the doctor today, and he told me I have the breasts of a 25-year-old."

The husband says, "Well, what did the doctor say about your 50-year-old ass?"

The wife replied, "Frankly dear, your name never came up."

Bud began to play better and became a friend.

> *"Because when they strike it can be that quick that if they're within range, you're dead, you're dead in your tracks. And his head weighs more than my body so it's WHACK!*
>
> -Steve Irwin

The Port Labelle Inn and Oxbow Golf Club near the Florida Everglades has signs on the course, "Do Not Molest the Alligators."

What the hell? Do they think golfers will jump on the backs of alligators and poke and tease them?

*

A judge in Florida heard a Motion to Dismiss on a complaint of a golfer who'd been bitten by a rattlesnake looking for his ball in the rough and later filed suit against the golf course for damages.

The snake bitten Plaintiff's lawyer argued, "Your honor, the golf course should have had, in the very least, a simple warning sign, "Beware of poisonous snakes."

The judge considered it a second, then said, "If I rule the Plaintiff has a right to sue in this case, then that would require every golf course in the State of Florida to post a sign, 'Beware of Rattlesnakes?'

Well, everyone knows there's poisonous snakes in Florida. Do hammer manufacturers have to put labels on hammers – "If you hit your thumb with this, it will hurt you?"

Case dismissed."

*

A tourist played a golf course in Northern Queensland. After hitting his drive to the right of the fairway into rough tall grass and bushes, which Aussies call "Bush", the golfer drove his cart to where his ball went in and walked in to look for his ball.

As the two Aussies he was playing drove up, one of them shouted, "Hold on, mate!"

"What? I'm just gonna to take a quick look for my ball."

The Aussies chuckled.

"What?" The tourist asked.

"That's a funnel web spider (dangerous poisonous spider – big as your hand, fangs, hairy, etc.) web right next your arm, mate. There's a female spider in the web and there should be a male – you don't want to meet it – somewhere on the ground."

"Are they dangerous?"

Both Aussies were laughing now, "You've got to respect the nature here, mate."

*

A guy walks into a bar with an alligator ten feet long and sits down at the bar.

"Hey! You can't bring that in. Get it out of here before it chews somebody's leg off!" The bartender tells him.

"Oh, no. It's a tame alligator. Wouldn't hurt a fly. Here let me show you." The golfer slaps a nearby bench and the alligator slowly crawls up on the bench. Then the guy unzips his pants and sticks his dick in the alligator's mouth. The alligator just lays there with his mouth open for a few minutes, then the golfer pulls his dick out and zips up.

"See, this gator is tame. Anybody else what to try this?" Said the golfer.

A drunk at the end of the bar stumbles over and says, "Yeah, I'd like to try that, but I can't keep my mouth open that long."

"Demand money with a threat of violence and you'll go to jail. Do it with a threat of eternal damnation, and it's tax deductible."

-Steve Hofstetter

A husband and wife attend a small service at the local church totally packed with worshippers on Sunday before going to golf for their usual Sunday game. It was hard to find seats but they eventually squeezed in a back pew.

The preacher spoke of patience in life, nothing comes easy, good things take time and we should always try to act and speak properly as proper ladies and gentlemen.

The man was very moved by the preacher's sermon, so he stopped to shake the preacher's hand.

"Reverend, that was the best damn sermon I ever did hear! Not only is it good advice for life, but a good temperament to keep when playing golf."

The Reverend replied, "Oh! Why, thank you sir, but please, I'd appreciate it if you didn't use profanity in the Lord's house."

"I'm sorry Reverend, but I can't help myself… it was such a damn good sermon!"

The Reverend replied, "Sir, please, I cannot have you behaving this way in Church!"

"Okay Reverend, but I just wanted you to know that I thought it was so damn good, that I put $5,000 in the collection plate."

The Reverend's eyes opened wide as he remarked, "No Shit! Haha! You motherfucka! Bring all your friends next Sunday and I'll get these other bastards out of here!"

Lawyer: "This myasthenia gravis -- does it affect your memory at all?"

Witness: "Yes."

Lawyer: "And in what ways does it affect your memory?"

Witness: "I forget."

Lawyer: "You forget? Okay, can you give us an example of something that you've forgotten?"

A defendant in a lawsuit involving large sums of money was saying to his lawyer, "If I lose this case, I'll be ruined."

"It's in the judge's hands now," said the lawyer.

"What does this judge like?"

"Well I know he'd rather be golfing than sitting on the bench. He loves golf. What are you getting at?" Asked the lawyer.

"Would it help if I sent the judge a gross of the finest golf balls?" asked the defendant.

"Oh no!" said the lawyer. "This judge is a stickler for ethical behavior. A stunt like that would prejudice him against you. He might even find you in contempt of the court. In fact, you shouldn't even smile at the judge."

After a while, the judge rendered his decision and decided in favor of the defendant.

As the defendant left the courthouse in a very glad mood after hearing the favorable decision, he said to his lawyer, "Thanks for the tip about the golf balls. It worked."

"I'm sure we would have lost the case if you'd sent them," said the lawyer.

"But I did send them," said the defendant.

"What?? You did?"

"Yes, That's how we won the case."

"I don't understand," said the lawyer.

"It's easy. I sent a sleeve of the cheapest golf balls I could find to the judge, but enclosed the plaintiff's business card."

"Arguing with a lawyer is like wrestling a pig in the mud. Sooner or later you realize they enjoy it."

-Anonymous

One for the Clubhouse bar:

A man walks into a golf clubhouse bar. He sees a very sharp looking woman wearing the latest golf fashions sitting on a bar stool all alone. He walks up to her and says, "Hi there, how's it going tonight?"

She turns to him, looks him up and down and then straight in the eyes and says, "I'll screw anybody at anytime, anywhere, day or night, in any country, your place or my place -- it doesn't matter to me."

The guy raises his eyebrows and says, "Really? What law firm do you work for?"

Golfwell's Fascinating Golf Stories and More Hilarious Adult Golf Jokes

"Golf is a game on how well you accept, respond to and score with your missed shots, much more so than it is a game of your perfect shots."

-Dr. Bob Rotella

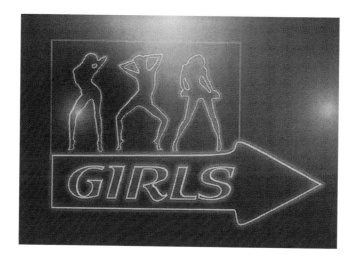

After Charlie retired, he played golf four times a week and neglected his wife. Being home alone a lot, the wife thought about getting a pet and decided she would like to find a talking and colorful macaw since it wouldn't be as much work as a dog or another pet and it would give her some company to hear it speak.

She went to a pet shop and immediately spotted a large beautiful macaw with red blue and yellow colors. She asked how much the bird costs.

The pet shop owner said it was just $25.

Delighted that such a rare looking and beautiful bird was so cheap, she decided to buy it.

But, the owner looked at her and said, "Look, I should warn you this beautiful bird used to live in a whorehouse. Sometimes it says some very vulgar and rude stuff."

The woman wondered about this for a while, then finally decided to buy the bird, and the pet shop owner sold her the bird and she took it home. She hung the bird's cage up in her living room and waited for it to say something. The bird looked around the room, then at her, and said, "New house, new madam."

The woman was a bit shocked at the implication, but then thought, "That's not so bad."

A few minutes later, the woman's three teenage daughters returned from school. When they looked over the bird, the bird looked back at them and said, "New house, new madam, new whores."

The three girls and their mother were taken aback by this, but then they all began to laugh it off. Then a few hours later, Charlie came home from golf. husband came home from golf.

The bird looked at him and said, "New house, new madam, new whores, same old faces. Hi Charlie!"

"This fitness thing is blown out of proportion. What am I going to do on a treadmill - smoke a cigarette and drink a diet Coke?"

-John Daly

Another one for the Clubhouse bar:

Two very old men were sitting next to each other in the clubhouse bar.

After a while, one looks at the other and says, "I can't help but think, from listening to you, that you're from Ireland ...."

The other responds proudly, "Yes, I sure am!"

The first one says, "So am I! And whereabouts in Ireland are ya from?"

The other answers, "I'm from Dublin, I am."

The first one responds, "So, am I. And what street did you live on in Dublin?"

The other says, "A lovely little area. It was in the west end. I lived on Maple Place in the central of town."

The first one says, "Faith, and it's a small world. So did I! So did I! And what school did ya go to?"

The other answers, "Well now, I went to Holy Heart of Mary, of course...."

The first one gets really excited and says, "And so did I! Tell me, what year did ya graduate?"

The other answers, "Well, now, let's see. I graduated in 1952."

The first old guy almost falls off his barstool and shouts out, "The Good Lord must be smiling down upon us! Saints be praised! I can't believe our good luck at winding up in the same pub tonight! Can you believe it? I graduated from St. Mary's in 1959 meself!"

About this time, a lady walks into the bar, sits down, and orders a drink.

Mary, the bar maid, walks over to her shaking her head and mutters, "It's going to be a looong night."

"Why do you say that, Mary?"

"The Murphy twins are totally inebriated again."

"A good marriage would be between a blind wife and a deaf husband."

-Michel de Montaigne

Little Billy came home from school to see the families pet rooster dead in the front yard. It was flat on its back with its legs sticking straight up in the air.

When his Dad came home Billy said, "Dad our rooster's dead and his legs are sticking in the air. Why are the rooster's legs sticking in the air?"

His father thinking quickly said, "Son, that's so God can reach down from the clouds and lift the rooster straight up to heaven."

"Gee Dad that's great," said little Billy.

A few days later, Dad comes home from his usual Saturday golf round, Billy rushed out to meet him yelling, "Dad, Dad, we almost lost Mom today!"

"What do you mean?" said Dad.

"Well, when I got home from school early today and went up to your bedroom and there was Mom flat on her back with her legs in the air screaming, 'Jesus I'm coming, I'm coming.' If it hadn't of been for Uncle George holding her down we'd have lost her for sure!"

8. MORE JOKES FOR THE CLUBHOUSE BAR (The Wrong Assumption)...

"The only thing worse than being blind is having sight but no vision."

-Helen Keller

It can be annoying when someone assumes the wrong thing...except when it's funny.

The head nun tells the two new nuns that they must paint their room without getting any paint on their clothes.

So, the one nun says to the other, "Hey, let's take all our clothes off, fold them up, and lock the door."

So, they do this, and begin painting their room.

Soon they hear a knock at the door. They ask, "Who is it?"

"Blind man!"

The nuns look at each other, then one nun says, "He's blind, he can't see. What could it hurt."

They let him in.

The blind man walks in and says, "Hey, nice tits. Where do you want me to hang the blinds?"

"Your assumptions are your windows on the world. Clean them off every once in a while, or the light won't come in."

-Isaac Asimov

A beautiful blonde woman walks into the doctor's office and the doctor is infatuated by how stunning she looks. She played golf regularly and was in excellent shape. She had more curves than Bubba Watson's golf ball drawing or fading in flight.

All his professionalism goes right out the window...

He tells her to take off her pants.

She does, and the doctor starts rubbing her thighs.

"Do you know what I am doing," asks the doctor?

"Yes, checking for abnormalities." she replies.

He tells her to take off her blouse and bra. She takes them off.

The doctor begins rubbing her breasts and asks, "Do you know what I am doing now?"

She replies, "Yes, checking for cancer."

Finally, he tells her to take off her panties, lays her on the table, gets on top of her and starts making love to her.

He says to her, "Do you know what I am doing now?"

She replies, "Yes, getting herpes -- that's why I am here!"

"What an incredible Cinderella story! This unknown, he comes out of nowhere… to lead the pack at Augusta. He's at the final hole. He's about 375 yards away, he's gonna hit about a 2-iron, I think. (Bill Murray swings and pulverizes a flower). Oh, he got all of that.

The crowd is on its feet at Augusta. The normally reserved Masters crowd is going wild… for this young Cinderella, he's come out of nowhere. He's got about 370 yards left, he's going to hit about a 5-iron, it looks like. He's got a beautiful backswing… (Bill Murray swings and pulverizes another flower) that's -- oh, oh he got all of that one! He's gotta be pleased with that!

The crowd is just on its feet here. Here's the Cinderella boy. Tears in his eyes as he lines up this last shot. He's got about 210 yards left, and he's got a, looks like he's got an 8-iron. This crowd has gone silent… Cinderella story, out of nowhere, this former greenskeeper, about to become the Masters champion (Bill Murray swings and pulverizes a flower). It looks like a mirac – oh, it's in the hole! It's in the hole!

-Bill Murray (Carl Spackler) from Caddyshack

A guy was standing in a bar and a guy sits down next to him. After a while they get to talking and at about 10:00 pm the second guy says,

"Oh well, I better get home. My wife doesn't like me to stay out during late night."

The first guy replies, "I'll help you out of this. I do this all the time when I'm out too late golfing. Just do what I say. Go home. Sneak into the bedroom. Pull back the covers. Get down and put your head between her legs then lick, lick and lick for about 20 minutes and there will be no complaints in the morning."

The guy's not sure what to do but nods his head agreeing, and continues to drink for another hour before heading home to give it a try.

When he gets home, the house is pitch black.

He sneaks upstairs into the bedroom, pulls back the covers and proceeds to lick for 20 minutes.

The bed is like a swamp. He decides to get up and wash his face.

As he walks into the bathroom, his wife is sitting on the toilet.

Seeing her, he screams, "What the hell are you doing in here?!"

"Quiet!", she exclaims. "You'll wake my mother."

"I believe that imagination is stronger than knowledge. That myth is more potent than history. That dreams are more powerful than facts. That hope always triumphs over experience. That laughter is the only cure for grief…."

-Robert Fulghum

For the clubhouse bar:

A total naked woman rushed into a taxi.

The taxi driver turned back and stares at her not saying anything.

The woman asked the taxi driver, "Why are you staring at me that way, haven't you ever seen a naked woman?"

The taxi driver replied, "No, I just wonder where you keep your money?"

9. LYDIA KO (Growing Up Near Auckland)

"If I feel anxious every time someone is staring at me, well, I can't control what they stare at, but my reaction is, I'm just not going to go outside the house. I'm going to stay in and chill. And when I do go out, I understand what comes along with that."

- Tom Brady

Lydia Ko: A Winner

By Don from the Team at Golfwell

Lydia grew up in Auckland's Northshore. As she grew from a child to a teen, she kept winning amateur events and eventually became the number one amateur in the world.

My wife and I came to New Zealand in 2006 and didn't know anything about Lydia. We liked golf and the culture here so we settled here and joined the Gulf Harbour Golf Club about 45 min north of Auckland and a world class golf course then ranked #9 in New Zealand.

Lydia began learning golf at the age of five coached by Kiwi, Guy Wilson. When she reached her teens, she joined Gulf Harbour and practiced there every day. My wife and I, as well as everyone at Gulf Harbour, got to know her and her family.

Lydia began playing LPGA events as an amateur and due to her constant traveling, she wasn't around Gulf Harbour much. But, before she became a pro, the Club arranged to give her a Sendoff Reception to wish her all the best.

At the reception, I talked at length with Lydia and her coach, Guy Wilson. I told them the well-known story on how the great Jack Grout (who coached the young Jack Nicklaus) disagreed with those that regarded him the greatest golf coach ever since he taught Jack Nicklaus.

Grout would say, "Well I told Jack to hit a draw, he did it perfectly. When I told him to hit a fade, or a straight shot, again, he did it all perfectly. I didn't feel I was Jack's coach, I just shared what I knew and Jack just simply did it effortlessly."

Guy Wilson laughed, and said he could relate to that. Lydia laughed too in her very relaxed and laid back manner. She knew she was a very good golfer but that's just the way she was and didn't think that was anything overly special.

Tom Grady's quotation which precedes this story isn't a story you would hear about the Kiwis living in New Zealand since Kiwis treat everyone the same. It's a society where everyone gets the same respect from janitors to the Prime Minister.

Kiwis put a high value respect for others. I've seen men take off their hats and smile allowing ladies to pass by. Walt Disney would have loved New Zealand as the spirit of his personally designed town, Celebration, near Walt Disney World in Orlando, already existed here in this small country of four million in the South Pacific.

Kiwi's understand celebrities want their privacy and respect that. For example, my wife and I were in Wellington at the Portofinos Restaurant on the waterfront, and I looked out in the harbour and saw a large sailing yacht turn in the wind and noticed the name "Suri" on it.

"That's Tom Cruise's Boat," I said to my wife. My wife didn't know what I was talking about.

I asked our waitress, "Isn't that Tom Cruise's yacht?"

"Yes, it is. He and Peter Jackson are sitting over there," she said, slightly nodding her head in their direction.

I looked across the room and against the wall, and there were Peter Jackson and Tom Cruise sitting by themselves. Other people at nearby tables paid no attention to them. Nobody was interrupting them (I assume they were probably discussing movie work), and no one in the restaurant stared at them or sought autographs, or took photos, selfies, etc.

As anyone gets to be a celebrity, privacy gets scarce. Richard Gere in his heyday was so tired of being hounded by everyone, he decided to take a two-week retreat to a remote part of India. He travelled through the jungle for a day to a very remote getaway. Upon finally arriving to the secluded far away resort, to his anguish, he was greeted by excited natives who kept yelling, "Officer and a Gentleman! Officer and a Gentleman!"

If things start to annoy you, have a laugh. Laughter helps you relax and refocus and is very beneficial for the psyche as a good golf joke tends improve your game as well as have a good time.

10. GOLF – FISH STORIES

True story:

Briny Baird, a retired PGA pro, kept a fishing rod in his golf bag. He was playing the TPC at Sawgrass years ago, while playing the par five 16th hole, he took a long look at the three-acre pond that runs down the right side (which also is the home of the infamous 17th Island green). He decided to take a few casts into the pond and pulled out his fishing rod.

"I moved off the green because I saw a golfer coming," said Baird.

Casting out, he hooked a nice fish. Tim Petrovic was in the group behind him and walked up just in time to help Baird haul in a seven-pound largemouth bass.

This is not true:

But what does Briny do after retirement? Some say he might be working in the fishing tackle department or a department store. Yeah right...here's the untrue story:

Briny was supposed to have been hired by a big department store. On his first day, the manager asked him, "Do you have any sales experience?"

Briny said, "Yes, I was a salesman back home in Miami."

Well, the boss liked Briny, so he hired him. "You start tomorrow. I'll come down after we close and see how you did."

Briny's first day on the job was rough but he got through it. After the store was locked up, the boss came down.

"How many sales did you make today?"

Briny says, "One."

The boss says, "Just one? Our sales people average 20 or 30 sales a day. How much was the sale for?"

Briny says, "$211,420.89."

Boss says, "$211,420.89? What the hell did you sell him?"

Briny says, "First I sold him a small fish hook. Then I sold him a medium fish hook. Then I sold him a larger fish hook. Then I sold him a new fishing rod. Then I asked him where he was going fishing, and he said down in the Keys, so I told him he was going to need a boat, so we went down to the boat department, and I sold him that twin-engine Boston Whaler. Then he said he didn't think his Honda Civic would pull it, so I took him down to the automotive department and sold him that 4X4 Blazer."

The boss said, "A guy came in here to buy a fish hook and you sold him a boat and truck?"

Briny says, "No, he came in here to buy a box of tampons for his wife, and I said, 'Well, since your weekend's shot, you might as well go fishing.'"

"Judge Smails: You know, you should play with me and Dr. Beeper. He's been club champion for four straight years and I'm no slouch myself.

Ty Webb: Don't sell yourself short, Judge, you're a tremendous slouch.

-Ty Webb (Chevy Chase) Caddyshack

Two golfers took the day off and decided to go fishing one early morning on Florida's Lake Okeechobee. One was constantly catching largemouth bass, one after another, but the other wasn't getting a nibble.

Finally exasperated, the other guy says, "Hey, how come you're getting so many fish and I'm not getting anything? What the hell am I doing wrong?"

"What are you using for bait?" The guy asks as he's reeling in another bass.

"Top water lures, spinners, spoons, other baits, worms. What are you using?" Said the other guy.

"Hell, that's stuff's out of date. You gotta use modern bait -- the right kind of bait to catch fish now-a-days."

"What are they eating then?" The other guy asks.

"Pussy man, pussy meat." The guy says with a grin.

"Pussy meat?! Where'd you get it from?"

"Well, I know a guy who's a strange butcher, really weird guy, strange, and he collects all kinds of pussies and sells it to me as fish bait. And man, it works like magic. Fish can't seem to get enough."

"Hmm..." said the other guy with a frown, "But I notice you keep sniffing the bait before you put it on the hook. Do you really have to smell the pussy?"

"Well," says the guy grinning. "The butcher's been hit in the head with a rock too many times -- he's not playing with a full deck – doesn't have both oars in the water, ya know?"

"Yeah, strange guy, so what?"

"Every now and then he tries to slip in an asshole."

11. AND THE MORAL OF THE STORY IS…(More jokes for the clubhouse bar)

"Turn the bullshit into goodshit."

-Anonymous

The Turkey and the Bull

When you pass through the entrance gate into the famous Cape Kidnappers Course in Hawkes Bay, New Zealand, (Ranked 33rd in the world), there is a fifteen-minute drive through magnificent scenery, cliffs, farmlands, and pastures to reach the Clubhouse.

There are farmlands adjacent to the course and a golfer hooks his drive into a pasture. Finding his ball, he couldn't help notice a turkey was chatting with a bull.

"I would love to be able to get to the top of that tree," sighed the turkey, "but I don't have the energy."

"Well, why don't you nibble on some of my droppings?" replied the bull. "They're packed with nutrients."

The turkey pecked at a lump of dung and found that it gave him enough strength to reach the first branch of the tree.

The turkey got down and after eating more dung, he reached the second branch. And so on until he was proudly perched at the top of the tree.

The golfer watched as a farmer approached angry at the turkey who wasn't supposed to be on the top of the tree, and the farmer shot the turkey out of the tree.

The golfer shook his head and said, "The moral of this story is: Bullshit might get you to the top, but it won't keep you there."

"I actually don't need to control my anger. Everyone around me needs to control their habit of pissing me off."
   -Anonymous

There once was a Native American who worked at an exclusive golf course in an Indian Reservation now developed into a large hotel and casino complex. His given name was "Onestone", so named because he had only one testicle.

Onestone hated his name. He asked everyone not to call him "Onestone".

But, they still called him Onestone, and after years and years of torment, Onestone finally went bezerk and said, "If anyone calls me Onestone again… I will kill them!"

No one dared call him "Onestone" any more.

Then one day a young woman named, Hummingbird, accidentally forgot and said, "Good morning, Onestone."

Onestone became enraged. He stood up and took her far, far away into a forest and kept making love to her all day and all night until she finally died of exhaustion.

The word got around that Onestone wasn't kidding and years went by and no one dared call him by his given name until a woman named Black Bird returned to the village after being away for many years.

Hummingbird, was Black Bird's cousin, and was overjoyed when she saw Onestone. She hugged him and said, "Hello, it's good to see you, Onestone."

Onestone grabbed her, took her deep into the forest, then he made love to her all day, made love to her all night, made love to her all the next day, made love to her all the next night, and the next day and night as well. But Black Bird wouldn't die!

And the moral of this story? You can't kill two birds with one stone.

"Oh Mrs. Crain, you wore green so you could hide from me. You're a little monkey woman. You're lean and you're mean and not too far in between, either, oh, I bet, are ya, are ya, huh? How'd you like to wrap your spikes around my head?"

    -Carl Spackler (Bill Murray) Caddyshack

I hit my ball into the water on the third hole, a par 3 on a course deep into the Canadian woods. I can't find my ball, so I assume it's in the hazard and start to measure two club lengths from the hazard line.

While I'm measuring, there is this fly flying over a pond. But while the fly was flying over the pond, there was a fish watching the fly and the fish said, "Shit, if that fly would just come down a little bit more, I could jump out and get the fly because I'm hungry."

But while the fish was watching the fly, there was a bear watching the fish watching the fly and the bear was like, "Shit, if that fly would just come down a little bit more the fish could get the fly, and I could get the fish because I'm hungry."

But while the bear was watching the fish watching the fly, there was a hunter watching the bear watching the fish watching the fly and the hunter was like, "Shit, if that fly would just come down a little bit more, the fish could get the fly, the bear could get the fish and I could get the bear because I'm hungry."

But while the hunter was watching the bear watching the fish watching the fly, there was a squirrel watching the hunter watching the bear watching the fish watching the fly and the squirrel was like, "Shit, if that fly would just come down a little bit more, the fish could get the fly, the bear could get the fish, the hunter could get the bear and I could go get his sandwich because I'm hungry."

But while the squirrel was watching the hunter watching the bear watching the fish watching the fly, there was a cat on a branch watching the squirrel watching the hunter watching the bear watching the fish watching the fly and the cat was like, "Shit, if that fly would just come down a little bit more, the fish could get the fly, the bear could get the fish, the hunter could get the bear, the squirrel could get his sandwich and I could get the squirrel because I'm hungry."

Anyway, the fly comes down, right? The fish gets the fly, the bear gets the fish, the hunter gets the bear, the squirrel gets the sandwich, and while the cat was trying to get the squirrel, the branch in the tree breaks and the cat comes crashing into the water.

The moral of this story is: When the fly comes down, the pussy gets wet.

"Watching Phil Mickelson play golf is like watching a drunk chasing a balloon near the edge of a cliff."

-David Feherty

At the end of class, little Sean's teacher asks the class to go home and think of a story to be concluded with, "The moral of the story is…."

The following day the teacher asks for the first volunteer to tell their story.

Little Suzy raises her hand.

"My dad owns a farm and every Sunday we load the chicken eggs on the truck and drive into town to sell them at the market. Well, one Sunday we hit a big bump and all the eggs flew out of the basket and onto the road."

When the teacher asked for the moral of the story, Suzy replied, "Don't keep all your eggs in one basket."

Little Lucy went next. "My dad owns a farm too. Every weekend we take the chicken eggs and put them in the incubator. Last weekend only eight of the 12 eggs hatched."

Again, the teacher asked for the moral of the story.

Lucy replied, "Don't count your chickens before they hatch."

Next up was little Sean. "My grandpa Rick took me golfing and let me drive the golf cart. We were going slow since there were four beginners who were older ladies and they wouldn't let us through.

"My grandpa asked them to let us play through but they ignored him. My grandpa called the pro shop to get someone to tell these ladies to get out of the way to let us go through, but no one answered the phone.

"My grandpa started drinking beer when a guy in the group behind us hit my grandpa Rick in the butt with his golf ball when he standing right in the middle of the fairway."

"My grandpa ran over to a groundskeeper who saw the whole thing and knocked him off his mower and jumped on it and drove the lawnmower over the guy's golf ball shredding it into little pieces.

"Then he jumped off the mower and gathered up the little pieces of golf ball and walked back to the guy that hit into us, pulled down his pants and shoved the golf ball pieces up his bottom.

"The groundskeeper was jumping up and down cheering my grandpa on. Then my grandpa took the guy's golf clubs and threw them into the lake. Then he drove the guy's golf cart into the lake. Then he threw the guy into the lake."

The teacher looked a little shocked. After clearing her throat, she asked what possible moral there could be to this story.

"Well," Sean replied, "Don't fuck with grandpa Rick when he's been drinking."

"Golf preparation: Back straight, knees bent, feet – a shoulder width apart. Form a loose grip. Keep your head down. Avoid quick backswing. Stay out of the water. Try not to hit anyone. Don't stand directly in front of the others. Quiet please, while others are preparing to go. Don't take extra strokes. Very good. Now flush the urinal and go outside and tee off."

-Sign in a Locker Room

At a golf course near Minneapolis, there was a bird who didn't fly south yet like the other birds. Winter was coming and he still flew around the golf course where there was plenty of food.

It was starting to get cold and the bird got caught up in a sudden blizzard so he tried to fly south and started off. He flew over farms but his wings froze and he plummeted to the ground below.

He knew he was a goner as he lay on the ground of a farm. Just then and a group of horses were coming his way and one of the horses, let out a pile of shit on the bird completely covering him up. The heat of the crap warmed him and defrosted his wings. Finally, the bird could breathe and move freely. Overjoyed, the bird began chirping and chirping totally ecstatic at his good fortune. A cat in a nearby bush heard the bird and pounced on the bird, swallowing him in one gulp.

Moral of the Story: Everyone who shits on you doesn't mean that their you're enemy. Everyone who gets you out of shit isn't necessarily your friend. And, if you're warm and happy in a pile of shit.... keep your mouth shut!

"If you are going to make a change, don't go halfway. Make it with conviction and stick with your new idea. Ignore the scoffers. Remember, it is a law of nature that if something is different you're going to be taunted, jeered, and told the world is flat. Let the doubters fall off the edge."

-Gary McCord, TV Golf Announcer

The tenth hole at The Players Club in Jacksonville, Florida has a stream running down the left side of the hole.

In a practice round, one player hit his ball near the stream. The others in the group walked down to help him find his ball.

While they were searching, a sausage floated down the stream apparently from the concession stand near the 10th tee.

They all didn't think much of it until a stray cat ran up and tried to get the sausage. The cat's paw got wet making the cat shy away.

A few seconds later a huge sausage floated by and the cat fell into the river trying to get it. They all watched in silence as the cat splashed around, finally scrambling out of the stream.

The moral is the story is: A big sausage makes the pussy wetter.

12. GOLFER NICKNAMES…And the Reasons for Them

"Annabeth: Hey, Seaweed Brain.

Percy: Will you stop calling me that?

Annabeth: You know you love it."

    -Rick Riordan

The Big Easy for Ernie Els: because he's big, and makes it look so easy.

The Big Wiesy: Michele Wie since she's six feet tall and her similar easy swing makes it look sooo easy.

Boom Boom for Fred Couples: Came from his easy swing but amazing distance off the tee.

Golden Bear for Jack Nicklaus: From his blond hair, large frame, aggressive play, and his success in golf and business; and he uses it as his logo. He has a large Sports Fishing yacht out of North Palm Beach bearing the Golden Bear emblem.

Great White Shark for Greg Norman: Big, blond, Australian former world no. 1. Ironically, despite the nickname and his prodigious number of tournament victories around the world, he is arguably more famous for the major championships he failed to win like the 1996 Masters, when he led by six shots going into the final round, but wound up five shots behind Nick Faldo. Jack, of course, leads with 19 runner ups in the majors with Greg having 8 runner ups in majors. The name "Great White Shark" sprung in 1981 during the 1981 Masters from a newspaper reporter.

The King for Arnold Palmer: To millions of adoring fans (Arnie's Army) he was simply the King, the most popular golfer of all time, who did much to create the modern game and its huge following, with a cavalier golf style and charismatic personality. Who else could win in such an exciting manner when he won his only US Open Title being followed by a huge throng of spectators, "Arnie's Army." One of his greatest victories, of course, was when he came from 7 strokes back, driving the green on the par four 346 yard green 1st hole at Cherry Hills as he began his final round. The Golden Bear was runner up.

Shrek for Louis Oosthuizen: His friends believe he resembles Shrek. His real name is 'Lodewicus Theodorus Oosthuizen,' after his grandfather.

The Lion, also known as "Long John" and "Wild Thing" for none other than John Daly: the cigarette-smoking, beer drinking, and a double major winner. He's been through divorces, alcoholism, fights and more, and goes on Tour in a mobile home - the 'Dalymobile'.

Tiger for Eldrick Woods: Tiger's father had a best friend with a South Vietnamese Colonel, Vuong Dang Phong. Phong's nickname was "Tiger." And Tiger was named after him.

13. BIG DICK GOLF JOKES

"I hate those e-mails where they try to sell you penis enhancers. I got ten just the other day. Eight of them from my girlfriend. It's the two from my mum that really hurt."
     -Jimmy Carr

Jim played a round of golf but couldn't concentrate and wound up shooting 114 being totally absorbed on whether or not he should propose to his girlfriend, Sandy.

He got frustrated thinking about it, so he bought a ring and went over to see her and got down on one knee and proposed.

Sandy, prior to her acceptance had to confess to Jim about her childhood illness.

She informed Jim that she suffered a disease, a breast growth disorder, that left her breasts almost nonexistent. She was completely flat chested.

He stated that it was okay because he loved her so much.

Jim smiled at Sandy and then hung his head down. "I too have a problem. My dick is the size of an infant and I hope you can deal with that when we re married," Jim confessed.

Sandy thought about it, then said, "Yes I will marry you and learn to live with your infant penis. It is you who I love, not your penis."

Sandy and Jim got married and were very eager to have sex -- they could not wait. So Jim whisked

Sandy off to their honeymoon hotel suite and they started touch teasing, and holding one another.

Sandy put her hands in Jim's pants. Then she began to scream and ran out of the room!

Jim ran after her to find out what was wrong.

She said, "You told me your penis was the size of an infant!"

"Yes, it is: 8 pounds, 7 ounces, 19 inches long!"

> *"Now go to bed, you crazy night owl! You have to be at NASA early in the morning. So, they can look for your penis with the Hubble telescope."*
>
> *-Tina Fey, Bossypants*

Three friends were having a drink after a golf round. They talked about sex and got into an argument on who was the best.

"My dick is so big, Stephen Hawkins invented a formula for it."

The next said, "My dick is so big, I even tried to measure it once, but the yard stick only went up to 36 inches."

The third said, "My dick is four inches…wide!"

They decided to bet each other $100 on who could make their wives scream more from sex.

They all went home to have sex with their wives. The next day they meet.

The first friend says, "I made love to my wife for 2 hours and she was screaming for at least 1 1/2 hours."

The second friend says, "That's nothing, I start licking my wife for two hours and she was screaming the whole time and half hour after that."

The third say, "That's nothing, I made love to my wife for ten minutes, I came a couple times I wiped my penis on the curtains and she still screaming."

Golfwell's Fascinating Golf Stories and More Hilarious Adult Golf Jokes

"When your mother asks, 'Do you want a piece of advice?' It's a mere formality as you well know it really doesn't matter if you answer, you're going to get the advice anyway."

-Erma Bombeck

Maria Spaghetti just got married to Tony Baloney, an up and coming amateur golfer, and being a traditional Italian, she was still a virgin. So, on her wedding night, she decided her and her new husband would stay at her mama's house and Maria was understandably very nervous.

But her mother reassured her. "Don't you worry, Maria. Tony's a very good man. Go upstairs, and he'll take care of you."

So up the stairs she went. When she got there, Tony took off his shirt and exposed his dark hairy chest.

Maria ran downstairs to her mother and says, "Mama, mama, Tony's got a big, dark hairy chest."

"Not to worry, Maria", says mama, "All very good men have dark hairy chests. Go on, go upstairs. He'll take very good care of you."

So, up the stairs she went. When she got upstairs she went into the bedroom, and Tony slowly took off his pants exposing his very dark hairy legs and Maria's eyes widened. Maria burst out of the room and went downstairs to talk to her mother.

"Mama, Mama, Tony took off his pants, and he's got hairy legs, too!"

"Don't you worry, Maria. All very good men have hairy legs. Tony's a very good man. Go upstairs now, and he'll take very good care of you."

So, up she went again. When she got up there, Tony took off his socks. On his left foot, he was missing three toes!

When Maria saw this, she ran downstairs.

"Mama, Mama, Tony's got a foot and a half!"

"Stay here and stir the pasta", says the mother, "this is a job for Mama!"

My dick is so big it has its own dick, and my dick's dick is bigger than your dick.
    - Drew Carey

A lady walked into the Texas Golf Course Clubhouse and saw a golfer with his boots propped up on an old chair.

He had the biggest boots she'd ever seen. The woman asked the man if it's true what they say about men with big feet are well endowed.

The golfer grinned and said, "Shore is, little lady. Why don't you come on out to the bunkhouse and let me prove it to you?"

The woman wanted to find out for herself, so she spent the night with him. The next morning, she handed him a $100 bill.

Blushing, he said, "Well, thankee, ma'am. Ah'm real flattered. Ain't nobody ever paid me fer mah services before."

"Don't be flattered. Take the money and buy yourself some boots that fit."

The phone beeps:

Jack: "Hello?"

Caller: "Is this Jack?"

Jack: "Yeah. Who's this?"

Caller: "What's got a little dick and hangs upside down."

Jack: "I don't know, what?"

Caller: "A bat."

Jack: "?"

Caller: What's got a big dick and hangs up?"

Jack: "I don't know."

Caller: (click)

    - Anonymous

Four guys who worked together had a regular tee time at 7 A.M. every Sunday. Unfortunately, one of the guys was transferred out of town, so the others began discussing how they would fill out the foursome.

A woman standing nearby couldn't help but overhear them and said, "Hey, I like to play golf and I've been looking for a regular foursome. May I join your group?"

The men hesitated, and told her she could play with them but only for one round, a trial round, and they would decide whether she could continue as a regular after the round.

She agreed and said, "I'll be there at 6:30 or 6:45." She showed up the next Sunday right at 6:30, and wound up shooting 65, a 7-under-par round.

The guys were happy and invited her to play with them every Sunday – for as long as she wanted.

"Ok, I'll be here at 6:30 or 6:45," she said.

The next Sunday, she showed up at 6:30 am. Only this time, she played left-handed and matched her 65 round of the previous week.

They all had drinks after the round and one of the guys asked her, "How do you decide if you're going to golf right-handed or left-handed?"

"That's easy." She said. Before I leave for the golf course, I pull the covers off my husband, who sleeps in the nude. If his dick is pointing to the right, I golf right-handed. If it's pointing to the left, I golf left-handed."

Another member of the group asked, "What if it's pointing straight up?"

She replied, "Then I'll be here at 6:45."

> *"We want to get the hell out of here. The quicker we clean up this Goddamned mess, the quicker we can take a little jaunt against the purple pissing Japs and clean out their nest, too, before the Goddamned Marines get all of the credit."*
>
> -General George Patton Jr.

One for the clubhouse bar:

The Department of Defense determined there were too many generals and offered senior generals an early retirement bonus package to any general who wanted to retire early:

As a special incentive, any general who retired early would get his full annual benefits plus $10,000 for every inch measured in a straight line between any two points on the general's body, and each general could select any pair of points he wished – a very long golden green parachute, so to speak.

The first man, an Air Force general, accepted. He asked the DOD Pension official to measure from the top of his head to the tip of his toes. He was six feet one inch tall so the good general walked out with a check for $730,000.

The second general who opted for an early retirement was an Army general. He requested them to measure from the tip of his outstretched hand to his toes. This came to eight feet one inch. So, the Army general received a check for $970,000.

When the third general, a seasoned and grizzled Marine general, was asked which points he wanted measured, he told the DOD Pension official to measure, "From the tip of my dick to the bottom of my balls."

The DOD pension official scratched his head. Then not wanting to insult the good general, he tactfully suggested perhaps the good Marine general might like to reconsider? He reminded the general of the very nice checks the other two generals just received.

But, the Marine general insisted. The DOD official reluctantly agreed but the marine general was told there would have to be a medical officer to do the measuring.

So, the medical officer asked the general to "Drop 'em." The marine general complied. The medical officer carefully started to measure with a measuring tape from the tip of the general's dick and began to measure back.

"My God!" the medical officer said, "Where are your testicles?"

The general replied, "In Vietnam."

Golf truth: "If you're afraid a full shot might reach the green while the group ahead of you is still putting out, you have two options: you can immediately shank a lay-up, or you can wait until the green is clear and top a ball halfway there."

-Anonymous

Another dick joke for the clubhouse bar:

A young woman buys a dusty old mirror at an antique shop from a gypsy, and hangs it on her bathroom door.

One evening, while she was getting undressed to take a bath, she jokingly chants, "Mirror, mirror, on my door, make my bust line forty-four. And kindly add a Double D so I can't see my golf ball teed".

Instantly, there was a flash brighter than a bolt of lightning and she watches the mirror and sees her breasts enlarge to huge beautiful breasts.

She's happy as can be and runs with her huge new bouncing and buxom breasts to tell her husband what happened. The husband is overjoyed and in minutes they both return.

The husband carefully crosses his fingers and says "Mirror, mirror on the door, make my penis touch the floor!".

Again, there's a bright flash of lightning...and his legs fall off.

14. JOKES FOR DELAYS ON THE COURSE, BACKUPS ON THE TEE OR ANYTIME (Keep a Good Mindset Going)

I was standing at the clubhouse bar one night minding my own business. This fat ugly chick came up behind me, grabs my ass and says, "You're kinda cute. You gotta phone number?"

I said, "Yeah, you gotta pen?"

She said, "Yeah, I got a pen."

I said, "You'd better get back in it before the farmer misses you."

Yeah, the doctor says I can take the cast off in six weeks.

I went to the drug store and told the clerk "Give me 3 packets of condoms, please."

Lady Clerk: "Do you need a paper bag with that, sir?

I said "Nah... She's pretty good lookin'....."

I was talking to a young woman in the clubhouse bar last night. She said, "If you lost a few pounds, had a shave and got your hair cut, you'd look all right.

I said, If I did that, I'd be talking to your friends over there instead of you.

Doctor says the constant flinching will stop in a few days and I'll be able to get back on the golf course real soon.

I was telling a woman in the clubhouse bar about my ability to guess what day a woman was born just by feeling her breasts.

"Really" she said, "Go on then... try."

After about 30 seconds of fondling she began to lose patience and said, "Come on, what day was I born?"

I said, "Yesterday."

The nurse says the 40 stiches will be taken out in seven days, but the case won't come off for eight weeks.

I went to the clubhouse bar last night and saw a big woman dancing on a table. I said, "Good legs."

She giggled and said, "Do you really think so?"

I said, "Definitely! Most tables would have collapsed by now."

I wasn't always hunched over like this, but I'll be back to normal soon.

Golf shot nickname: a "Mrs. Robinson:" You know you shouldn't take it on, but it's just too tempting.

-Anonymous

Bob, went on camping trip deep in the forest with his wife, kids, and mother-in-law.

One evening, just before going to bed for the night, Bob's wife looks around and realizes her mother is gone.

Rushing to her husband, she insists both of them try to find her mother right away. Bob picks up his 2 iron and gives his wife a 3 iron, then Bob takes a swig of whiskey, and Bob and his wife start to look for her.

In a clearing, not far from the camp, they see a dramatic, chilling sight. Bob's poor mother-in-law is backed up against a tree and a large Kodiak bear is standing up facing her and growling ferociously.

The wife cries out, "Bob, do something!"

Bob studies the drama and practice swings his 2 iron several times and says, "Shit, I'm not doing a damn thing. that poor bear got himself into this dangerous situation, so let him get himself out of it."

15. A GOLF STORY – Senior Ladies (We love them!) but they can be troublesome…

"You can tell a lot about a woman by her hands. For example, if they are placed around your neck she is probably slightly upset."

    -Anonymous

Years ago, I was playing golf on a small course in Florida when I accidently hit near 4 ladies playing in front of us.

In the past, I hadn't ever come close to hitting anyone. I was about 270 yards away from them on a par five and hit a 4 iron just trying to lay up on the par 5, but my ball must have hit a sprinkler head since it bounced super high in the air and in addition to that, there was a strong following wind which gusted behind me as soon as I hit it. My ball came to rest about 20 yards behind them.

They all heard my ball bounce and as if on cue they turned and looked at me and I felt like someone had turned on icy air conditioning to blast me.

I waved my apologies thinking foolishly that would be all that would be required. Two of them got in their cart, drove back to where I was standing and I learned from them I was the lowest form of life on the planet.

They didn't stop with a strong reprimand but called the pro shop and I was paid a visit by the ranger who further cautioned me, but at least I got an understanding look from the ranger telling me in so many words that although he didn't think it necessary, he had to go through the act of saying something since all four ladies ahead were watching him talk to me.

For the next four holes, they turned around and angrily look at me before they would take their shot while waving a hand or a naughty finger my way.

Life could, of course, be worse, and I thanked God I wasn't married to any of them.

But this was quite tame compared to what happened in July 2016 at the Buckingham Golf Club in the beautiful British Countryside which has a picturesque stream meandering through the course North of London.

It was allegedly reported in the Daily Mail that one member, Kaye, was in a relationship with Columb Harrington, the brother of Padraig Harrington, and Kaye was accused of falsifying her handicap. Kaye complained to the club about the false accusations.

That didn't do much good since soon after she complained, she got a letter posted on her club locker, "You bitch."

Didn't stop there, as she received an anonymous letter at her home, "If you're so unhappy perhaps you should join another club. We would like you to. You just like trouble."

Kaye boldly responded on her Facebook page saying she knew some members secretly didn't like her, "but I secretly know and don't give a F@#%"

Well said, I thought. But weeks went by and a window was smashed at the back of Kaye's home by someone using a golf club.

The brave police got up one of their biggest and bravest to actually warn two senior ladies' section members about bullying and harassment. Yes, that officer is still alive today and survived that ordeal.

16. ABSOLUTELY HILARIOUS GOLF JOKES

"You got to have the gut not to be afraid to screw up. The guys who win are the ones who are not afraid to mess up. And that comes right from the heart."
       -Fuzzy Zoeller

An ugly middle aged man staggers into the clubhouse bar and says, "Give me a triple of the strongest whiskey you got! Yeah, that 151 proof stuff there. Yeah, I'm so upset I can't even see straight!"

The club bartender say, "What happened to you John? Where are your glasses? You can't see anything without them?"

John gulps the drink down and says, "Give me another!"

The bartender begins to pour. "What the hell, John? You have a rough round?" Why you so upset?"

"Well, I finished my round and was walking off the eighteenth, when this gorgeous blonde slinks past me and motions me to follow her. I couldn't believe this was happening to me! Hey, I'm no movie star. So I leave my clubs in the cart and she and I go down the street to a nice hotel and up to her room. This was just too good to be true!"

"And then what happened?" Said the bartender.

"As soon as she shuts the door she slips out of her dress and she's completely naked. I take off my glasses and get out of my clothes! But as soon as I get into the bed, I hear a key card going in and the door handle jiggling!"

"Oh shit." Said the bartender.

"The blonde says 'Oh my lord, it's my husband! He must have lost his Martial Arts Championship match, he's going to go crazy! Quick, hide!'"

"Martial Arts Championship?" Said the bartender.

"So, I open the closet door, but that would be the first place he'd look, so I looked under the bed but that would be the second place he'd look, so it was all so blurry without my glasses, I stumbled around and the window was open, so I climbed out and hung outside holding on to the ledge, praying the guy wouldn't see me!"

The bartender says, "Wow, what did you do?"

"The guy comes in the room and says, "Who you been fucking now, bitch?'

"The blonde says, 'No-Nobody, honey! Come to bed and calm down.'

"Well, the guy starts tearing the room apart making a hell of a commotion! Sounded like he was tearing doors off, flipping up mattresses! I'm thinking, 'Boy, I'm glad I didn't hide in there.'

Then he shouts, 'Why's that window open?!' I think 'Shit! I'm dead now'. But the blonde is pleading him to stop looking."

"Good." Said the bartender.

"Well, my fingers are aching and I hear the guy go into the bathroom, and I hear water running for a long time, and I figure maybe he's going to shower, when all of a sudden the guy pours a pitcher of burning hot water out of the window right on top of my head! Shit he burned my face!"

The bartender says, "Oh shit, you must have been so mad you were going to take him on!"

"No, that didn't bother me. But then the guy then slams the window on my hands. I mean, Shit! Look at my fingers. They're a mess, I can hardly hold this glass."

"Yeah, John, your hands are a mess. I'd be so pissed I would have killed the guy. I see why you need these drinks!"

"No, I wasn't pissed. I could understand how the guy felt."

"What the hell?" The bartender said.

The bartender pour John his triple shot, then asks in exasperation, "Well, what did you get mad about?"

"Well I was hanging there, and I turned around and looked down, and I was only 4 fucking feet off the ground!"

From the movie, "Tin Cup"

Roy McAvoy: Well, I tend to think of the golf swing as a poem.

Romeo Posar: Ooh, he's doing that poetry thing again.

Roy McAvoy: The critical opening phrase of this poem will always be the grip, which the hands unite to form a single unit by the simple overlap of the little finger. Lowly and slowly the club head is led back, pulled into position not by the hands, but by the body, which turns away from the target, shifting weight to the right side without shifting balance. Tempo is everything, perfection unobtainable, as the body coils down at the top of the swing. There's a slight hesitation. A little nod to the gods.

Dr. Molly Griswold: A, a nod to the gods?

Roy McAvoy: Yeah, to the gods. That he is fallible. That perfection is unobtainable. And now the weight begins shifting back to the left, pulled by the powers inside the earth. It's alive, this swing! A living sculpture and down through contact, always down, striking the ball crisply, with character. A tuning fork goes off in your heart and your balls. Such a pure feeling is the well-struck golf shot. Now the follow through to finish. Always on line. The reverse C of the Golden Bear! The steelworkers' power and brawn of Carl Sandburg's Arnold Palmer!

Clint: Uh, he's doing the Arnold Palmer thing.

A guy out on the golf course took a high-speed ball right to the nuts. Writhing in agony, he fell to the ground. When he finally got himself to the doctor, he asked, "How bad is it, Doc? I'm going on my honeymoon next week and my fiancé is still a virgin."

The doctor said, "I'll have to put your penis in a splint to let it heal and keep it straight. It should be okay in about two weeks." Then the doctor took four tongue depressors and formed a neat little 4-sided bandage, and wired it all together; an impressive work of art.

The guy mentioned none of this to his girl and the two got married. On their honeymoon night, she opened her blouse to reveal a gorgeous set of breasts and told him, "You'll be the first; no one has ever touched these before."

The new bridegroom dropped his pants and said, "Look at this — it's still in the crate!"

"The difference between a good golf shot and a bad one is the same as the difference between a beautiful and a plain woman --a matter of millimeters."

-Ian Fleming, Goldfinger

A guy and his wife are out golfing one day when they come up to the hardest hole on the course; it goes way downhill and you can't quite see where your drive goes. So, they tee off and walk down the hill and, lo and behold, this guy's ball is right in front of a big barn.

The couple looks it over, and the wife says, "You know, if we open both barn doors, you will have a clear shot to the green."

The guy agrees, and they open both doors. He hits his ball and it makes it through the first set of doors but hits the far wall and comes ricocheting back—hitting his wife in the head and killing her.

A few months pass and he is out golfing again with his friends. They come up to the same hole and, wouldn't you know it, the guy's ball is right behind the barn again. One of his golf friends says, "You know, if we open both barn doors you will have a clear shot to the green."

The guy replies, "Nah, last time I tried that I got a 7."

*

The fourth hole of the Fort Myers Country Club in Florida is adjacent to Route 41. A golfer sliced his tee shot into moving traffic and his ball went through the windshield of a driver causing him to crash and he was killed.

The driver's estate sued the golfer and a jury awarded the driver's estate a judgment for $4,000,000.

After the verdict, the Plaintiff's lawyer asked the golfer what he was going to do about this?

The golfer replied, "Well, next time, I'm going to roll my right hand over more so I can see at least two knuckles on my right hand...."

"The greatest thing about tomorrow is, I will be better than I am today. And that's how I look at my life. I will be a better golfer, I will be a better person, I will be a better father, I will be a better husband, I will be a better friend. That's the beauty of tomorrow."

-Tiger Woods

A guy is suffering from severe headaches so he had to give up golf and really couldn't do very much as it was worse than a migraine and he suffered for years with no relief.

After going to several doctors and having various tests, he's finally referred to a headache specialist. The Specialist asks him what his symptoms are and he replies, "I get these blinding headaches; kind of like a knife across my scalp and..."

The doctor interrupts him, "And a heavy throbbing right behind the left ear?"

"Yes! Exactly! How did you know?"

"Well I am the world's greatest headache specialist, you know. But I, myself, suffered from that same type of headache for many years. It is caused by tension in the scalp muscles. This is how I cured it: Every day I would give my wife oral sex. When she came, she would squeeze her legs together with all her strength and the pressure would relieve the tension in my head. Try that every day for two weeks and come back and let me know how it goes."

Two weeks go by and the man is back. "Well, how do you feel?" the doctor asked.

"Doc, I'm a new man! I feel great! I haven't had a headache since I started this treatment! I can't thank you enough. And by the way, you have a lovely home."

"The uglier a man's legs are, the better he plays golf. It's almost a law."

-H.G. Wells

Two guys were just about to tee off on the first hole when a guy walks up carrying his bag and says, "Would you gentlemen mind my joining you? My partner didn't turn up."

"Yeah, sure. No problem." Both tell him.

As they are playing the round, one guy asks the newcomer, "So, what do you do for a living?"

"I'm a hitman"

"You're joking!" the guy said.

"No, I'm a hitman" he said. He reached into his golf bag, and pulled out a beautiful Martini Sniper's rifle having the latest telescopic sight. "What do you think of this baby?" Said the hitman.

"Do you mind my taking a look? I just want to see if I can see my house from here."

So, the picks up the expensive rifle and looks through the sight in the direction of his house.

"Yeah, I can see my house all right. This sight is fantastic! I can see right in the window. Wow! I can see my wife in the bedroom. Haha! I can see she's naked! Wait a minute. What the fuck?! That's my fuckin' neighbor with her!!

He turned to the hitman, "How much do you charge for a hit?"

"Since you were kind enough to let my play with you, I'll do a flat rate, one thousand dollars every time I pull the trigger."

"Can you do two for me now?"

"Sure, what do you want?"

"First, shoot my wife, she's always been nagging and bitching at me, so shoot her in the mouth. Then shoot the neighbor, he was supposed to be a friend of mine, but just shoot his dick off to teach him a lesson."

The hitman took the rifle and took aim, standing perfectly still for a few minutes.

"Are you going to do it or not?" said the guy impatiently.

"Just be patient man," said the hitman calmly, "I think I can save you a grand here...."

"It's easy to see golf not as a game at all but as some whey-faced, nineteenth-century Presbyterian minister's fever dream of exorcism achieved through ritual and self-mortification."

-Bruce McCall

After the 2016 Presidential Election, two Hillary Clinton supporters boarded a flight out of Washington, DC. One lady took a window seat and the other lady sat next to her in the middle seat.

Just before takeoff, a Trump supporter sat down in the aisle seat next to them.

After takeoff, the Trump guy kicked his shoes off, wiggled his toes and was settling in when the lady in the window seat said, "I need to get up and get a coke."

"Don't get up, Madam" said the man, "I'm in the aisle seat, I'll get it for you."

As soon as he left, one of the ladies picked up the Trump guy's shoe and spat in it.

When the Trump guy returned with the coke, the other lady said, "That looks good, I'd really like one, too."

Again, the Trump guy obligingly went to fetch it.

While he was gone, the other lady picked up the Trump guy's other shoe and spat in it.

When the Trump guy returned, they all sat back and enjoyed the flight.

As the plane was landing, the Trump guy slipped his feet into his shoes and knew immediately what had happened.

"Why does it have to be this way?" he asked. "How long must this go on? We don't want to be dividing our nation? This fighting needs to stop? This hatred? This animosity? This spitting in shoes and pissing in cokes?"

Calvin: "Cigars are all the rage, Dad. You should smoke cigars!"

Calvin's Mom interrupts: "Flatulence could be all the rage, but it would still be disgusting."

-Bill Watterson, There's Treasure Everywhere: A Calvin and Hobbes Collection

The captain of a golf club was a single guy who loved baked beans. He couldn't get enough even though he'd fart like hell. He'd be teeing up his ball and "Whoompf," he'd let out a huge fart. Others had to clear the tee until it dissipated.

He met a fine lady and wanted to marry her but kept telling himself she wouldn't marry him since he farts too much. He wanted this woman so he gave up his beloved baked beans and married her.

A few months into the marriage, the captain was driving back from the club and his car broke down on the way home. He called his wife and told her he'd be late and would walk the rest of the way and take care of the car later.

On the way home, he passed a restaurant featuring a special on baked beans and the aroma of freshly cooked baked beans was too much for him. He couldn't resist. He went in and ordered, and thinking he had about an hour walk left back to his house, he gulped down three extra-large helpings of beautiful baked beans thinking he'd blow out the gas while walking home.

So, he farted all the way home and by the time he got home, he thought he'd gotten rid of all the farts since he putt-putted all the way home.

His wife met him at the door excited. 'Darling, I've got a great surprise for you for dinner tonight. You're going to love it!'

She blindfolded him then led him to his chair at the head of the table telling him, "No peeking.".

He started to feel a fart coming on when the phone rang. His wife left him at the table and answered the phone.

While she was gone, he let loose a huge fart like a red hot and smokin' rotten egg.

Some say your own farts don't stink, but the captain was gagging and had a hard time breathing. He fanned the air and felt better but felt another one coming on. He shifted his weight and "Whoompf!"

It sounded like a tractor engine revving, and the air was tinted with a blue smoke. He wind milled his arms fanning the air hoping the smell would go.

His wife was still talking on the phone and he felt normal when another fart started to build and let go a winner. If farting was an Olympic event, he would have won the gold. The windows shook, the dishes on the table rattled, and heard the dog and cat rush out the door.

His farting continued for the next ten minutes. He fanned the air constantly with his napkin. When he heard the 'phone farewells,' he laid his napkin down folding his hands on top.

The captain was smiling now and was the picture of innocence when his wife returned.

She asked him if he'd peeked from his blindfold and he assured her he didn't. She removed his blindfold and yelled, "'Surprise!"

To his dismay, shock and horror, there were ten dinner guests seated around the table for his surprise birthday party.

"You know I need that cockiness, the self-belief, arrogance, swagger, whatever you want to call it, I need that on the golf course to bring the best out of myself. But, you know, once I leave the golf course, that all gets left there."

- Rory McIlroy

A man was rushed into the emergency room needing surgery on his penis.

The ER physician examined him and asked, "What the hell happened?"

"Well, doc, I've been a member of the Fireside Golf Club for several years and there's this beautiful blond waitress in the clubhouse. She's blonde and built, a beautiful and curvaceous woman. She's got a problem since she's so horny that every time she goes back in the kitchen, she masturbates with a sausage. She sticks it in a hole on a bench, then she goes up and down and masturbates herself on it."

"And?" asked the doctor.

"Well, I felt this was a lot of wasted pussy, so I got under the bench and when she put the sausage in the hole, I removed it and substituted my dick."

"It was a great idea and everything was going well. Then someone came in the kitchen and she tried to hide by taking a hammer pretending she was tenderizing it for the skillet."

"Show me a man who is a good loser and I'll show you a man who is playing golf with his boss."

    - James Patrick Murray

Another one for the clubhouse bar:

A Problem:

Ten blondes and a brunette were hanging onto a rope that was tied to an airplane. They knew that one of them needed to let go because the weight of all eleven of them would tear the rope and they would all die.

So, they argued back and forth about who was to let go. This went on for a few minutes, until the brunette finally said, "Ok, I'll let go!"

The brunette gave a little speech about why she would go and said her farewells. All the blondes were so touched, they started clapping.

Problem solved.

"Golf has probably kept more people sane than psychiatrists have."

- Harvey Penick

Her husband went out to play golf, so his blonde wife decides to try horseback riding, even though she's never had lessons – a brand new experience for her.

She boldly mounts the horse and the horse all at once starts in motion.

The horse gallops along at a steady and rhythmic pace. The blonde starts to slip from the saddle. Terrorized, she grabs for the horse's mane, but misses then grabs it a second time but can't get a firm grip. She finally throws her arms around the horse's neck, but slides down the side of the horse anyway holding on to the horn of the saddle.

The horse gallops along, seemingly oblivious to its slipping rider. She tries to leap off away from the horse and jump to safety.

But, her foot has become entangled in the stirrup! She is dragged and the horse gallops along with pounding hooves as her head is struck against the ground again and again.

She almost passes out as her head is battered against the ground, crying desperately for help until Joe, the Wal-Mart manager runs out to shut the horse off.

"Laughter is wine for the soul - laughter soft, or loud and deep, tinged through with seriousness - the hilarious declaration made by man that life is worth living."

-Sean O'Casey

For the clubhouse bar:

During a long flight home after watching a golf tournament and drinking a lot of beer, a guy developed a serious problem. He made several attempts to get into the men's room, but found it to be occupied each time. The flight attendant noticed that he was walking funny, taking small steps and had a look of anxiety on his face.

"Sir" she said, "the ladies' room is unoccupied. You may use it if you promise not to touch any of the buttons on the wall."

At that point he would have promised anything!

He went to the ladies' room, relieved himself, and sat there savoring the relief. He noticed the buttons he'd promised not to touch. The buttons were labeled "WW", "WA", "PP", and the red one was labeled "ATR".

Who would know if he touched them? He couldn't resist! The curiosity was too great!

He pushed the button labeled "WW". Warm water was sprayed gently upon his bottom. Such a contented feeling came over him!

"Men's rooms don't have things like this," he thought.

Anticipating even greater pleasure, he pressed the button labeled "WA". Warm air replaced the warm water. It dried his underside thoroughly. The warm air stopped.

Without hesitation, he pressed the "PP" button. A large powder puff caressed his bottom adding the fragrant scent of spring flowers to his unbelievable pleasure.

"The ladies' room is more than a restroom," he thought, "this is a place of tender loving care!"

When the powder puff had quit, he pushed the red button marked "ATR" knowing this must be the ultimate joy in the ladies' room experience!

The next thing he knew he was in the hospital when he opened his eyes. A nurse was staring at him.

"What happened? How did I get here? The last thing I remember, I was in the ladies' room on the plane."

The nurse replied, "you pushed too many buttons, Sir. The last button, marked 'ATR', was an automatic tampon remover ...... your penis is under your pillow."

Golfwell's *Fascinating Golf Stories and More Hilarious Adult Golf Jokes*

"The difference between sex and love is that sex relieves tension and love causes it."

-Woody Allen

Once upon a time, a woman complained to her doctor that her husband was golfing all the time. He competed on the club team, entered every tournament, and literally gave her up for golf. She and her husband had stopped having any sex.

So, the doctor gave her a bottle of pills and told her to put them in his drink and she would be 'satisfied.'

The woman could hardly believe the doctor but put one pill in his morning coffee and that evening they romantically kissed for 10 minutes.

The next morning, she put two pills in his coffee, and that evening, they kissed and caressed each other for 20 minutes.

The next day, she said, "What the hell," and put the entire bottle in his morning coffee.

A few days later, the doctor's office called to check on her progress.

The woman's housekeeper answered the phone. When the doctor's nurse enquired how she was doing, the housekeeper replied, "She's dead; so is the neighbor's wife, my asshole hurts, and the husband is out naked on the front lawn yelling 'Here kitty, kitty.'"

"I have made really some significant deals because I play golf."

-Donald Trump

For the clubhouse bar:

During the last Presidential Election, Hillary had to work through all the stress related to the Benghazi hearings and unsecure emailing.

At a meeting where she was discussing these very stressful issues she took a bathroom break. When she went inside, she was approached by a lady reporter.

"Hillary, I'm on your side but those are some tough issues you're dealing with. I sympathize with all that you're going through. I have some inside news on these issues which may give you a boost to gain more votes and you'll win this election. They won't be able to touch you."

"What are you talking about?" said Hillary.

"I've got inside information on your emails and the hacking going on."

"Okay, what have you got?" Said Hillary.

"Well, I first need to ask you something for my column, an exclusive story?"

"Okay, you got it." Said Hillary.

"Have you ever given Bill oral sex? A blow job?"

A bit shocked, Hillary paused, the replied wryly, "Yes, but I didn't swallow".

Now that Donald Trump has won the Presidency, it's probably the first time a non-politician and successful business man has won, but it's most likely not the first time, Trump has pushed a black family out its home.

17. KEEP LAUGHING

"Laugh, even when you feel too sick or too worn out or tired. And keep laughing, even though you're trying not to cry and the tears blur your sight… So, don't live life in fear. Because after going through all the crap, you are stronger now."

-Alysha Speer

A friend of mine named Charlie once told me around the time of the US Open Tennis Tournament, "I know, Novak Djokovic and we are buddies."

I said, "Sure you are."

He said, "No, really! Come with me." They take a plane to Monte Carlo and Charlie goes up to this huge mansion and knocks on the door. Novak answers and says,

"Charlie! Come on in!" and Novak puts his arm around Charlie.

I was amazed.

Not long after that, I was talking to Charlie about Donald Trump.

"I know Donald," Charlie said.

"Yeah right, Charlie."

"C'mon I'll show you," Charlie said. They get on a plane and fly to New York City. The doorman at the Trump Tower Residences greeted us,

"How the hell you doing, Charlie?" said the doorman.

We take the elevator all the way up and Donald greets us as we get off the elevator and gives Charlie a big hug and invites us in.

This was getting surreal. Charlie seemed to know everyone!

I tested Charlie with a few more people. We were back in Washington DC and Charlie was telling me he was buddy-buddy with Jack Nicklaus, Jordan Spieth, and Barrack Obama.

"You're full of shit, Charlie. You don't know Obama.

"Oh, yes I do." We went to hear Obama give a Press Conference, and just before he started answering questions, he said,

"Hey, I see my friend Charlie out there. Let's have a beer, Charlie, after this."

Same kind of thing happened when we went to Vladimir Putin's house and got through security -- even the security guards knew Charlie. Putin answered the door, and said "Charlie!" and gave my friend a big hug, and invited us in for drinks.

Charlie must indeed know everyone, I thought.

One day we were having another conversation and Charlie said something about "my friend the Li Keqiang."

I said, "Charlie, you don't know the Premier of China? He doesn't deal with Westerners?"

"Wanna bet?" Said Charlie.

So, we flew to Tiananmen Square in Beijing. We were standing in the big crowd waiting for Li Keqiang to address the crowd.

Charlie said, "Excuse me for a little while" and disappeared into the crowd.

A little while after that, Li Keqiang appeared on the balcony and held up his arms. The crowd cheered!

And who should come out to the balcony next? Charlie came out and the crowd cheered even louder!

I looked to my left and asked the guy next to me what he thought of all this and he said, "Who's that guy up there with Charlie?"

"Perhaps more than any other sport, golf focuses pressure on the player. There are no time constraints, as there are in other sports. Your competitors are not allowed to hinder you, as they are in other sports. The pressure originates in yourself; it builds from doubts. A two-foot putt on the practice green doesn't spark many doubts. A two-foot putt to win a bet or a tournament or a Masters is another thing entirely."

-Joe Posnanski, The Secret of Golf: The Story of Tom Watson and Jack Nicklaus

A man walks into a sperm bank and declares, "I'm one of the wealthiest men in the world and have an I.Q. of 165, I'd like to make a donation."

The nurse gives him a sealed cup and directs him to a private room. Twenty minutes later the man hasn't come out, the nurse knocks on the door. "Is there a problem?"

"I'm sorry, I'm so embarrassed, I used my right hand. I used my left hand. I poured cold water on it and hot water on it. I banged it against the counter, I shook it…. Could you help me?

The nurse replied "I don't usually do this but it would be my pleasure."

She gets on her knees and begins to blow him.

"Nurse, now I'm not saying I don't really appreciate this, but I just need help getting the cap off the jar."

The Ryder Cup:

"I trust that the effect of this match will be to influence a cordial, friendly and peaceful feeling throughout the whole civilized world… I look upon the Royal and Ancient game as being a powerful force that influences the best things in humanity."
   -Samuel Ryder

Eh? This might be a more accurate description:

"It would be very easy to drool with sentimentality over the Ryder Cup. But, at the end of the day, it is simply two teams trying to knock seven bells out of each other, in the nicest possible way."
   -Peter Alliss

A story about the different abilities we each have:

On a very small farm, a farmer lived with his wife and the farmer and his wife had three sons. They were not financially well off, in fact they were very poor and just had a single cow on their small farm.

The wife of the farmer woke up early in the morning and checked on the cow and saw it was stone cold dead and lying in the field with its four legs sticking up in the air. She became depressed and despondent. How could they possibly continue to feed her family? In a depressed state of mind, she hung herself.

When the farmer woke up seeing both his wife and the cow dead, he began to see the hopelessness of the situation, and shot himself in the head.

The first son got up and saw both of his parents were dead and he saw the dead cow as well. He got depressed and despondent and yes, he also decided life was no longer worth living and went down to the river to drown himself but when he got there, he saw a mermaid sitting on the bank. He couldn't believe his eyes.

She said, "I'm a magical mermaid and I know the reason for your despair. If you will have sex with me five times in a row, I will restore your parents and the cow to you." The son agreed to try, but couldn't have any more sex after four times so the mermaid let him drown himself in the river.

Next the second oldest son woke up. He became depressed and despondent and started off to the river to end it all. The mermaid greeted him as well and said to him, "If you will have sex with me ten times in a row, I will make everything right." And while the son tried his best (seven times!), the mermaid let him drown himself in the river.

The youngest son woke up and saw everyone dead. He became despondent and walked down to the river to throw himself in. And there he also met the mermaid.

"I am a magical mermaid and understand how you feel. I can make everything right if you will only have sex with me fifteen times in a row."

The young son replied, "Is that all? Why not twenty times in a row?"

The mermaid was taken aback by this request.

Then he said, "Hell, why not twenty-five times in a row?" And even as she laid back agreeing to his request, he said, "Why not THIRTY times in a row?"

"Enough!" She said. "Okay, if you will have sex with me thirty times in a row, then I will bring everybody back to perfect health."

Then the young son asked, "Wait! How do I know that thirty times in a row won't kill you like it did the cow?"

"Golf? A passion, an obsession, a romance, a nice acquaintanceship with trees, sand and water."

-Bob Ryan

For the Clubhouse bar:

One day The Lord came to Adam to pass on some news.

"I've got some good news and some bad news," The Lord said.

Adam looked at The Lord and said, "Well, give me the good news first."

Smiling, The Lord explained, "I've got two new organs for you. One is called a brain. It will allow you to create new things, solve problems, and have intelligent conversations with Eve.

The other organ I have for you is called a penis. It will give you great physical pleasure and allow you to reproduce your now intelligent life form and populate this planet.

Eve will be very happy that you now have this organ to give her children."

Adam, very excited, exclaimed, "These are great gifts you have given me. What could the bad news possibly be?"

The Lord looked upon Adam and said with great sorrow, "You will never be able to use these two gifts at the same time."

For those who take shit from all sides and those that give shit to all sides:

A Story by a caddie about his caddie master, Dick Millweed:

"The mornings came hard, and our caddie master, Dick Millweed, had a temper that could make a hangover seem like a seismic fracture.

He was a small man with a soft, friendly voice. He was not intimidating at all, until he lost it.

In his defense, he took shit from all sides - from the members who wanted their favorite caddie and their preferred tee time, from the golf staff who wanted him to perform a million menial duties, and from us when we showed up bleary eyed and incoherent and sometimes didn't show up at all.

And there was hell to pay if a caddie should stumble in late, because then Millweed's lips would begin to tremble and his blue eyes would explode from his head and grow big like huge saucers and he appeared to grow with them. It was like some shaman or yogi trick.

Pound for pound, I've never met anyone else who could so effectively deliver anger. He would yell, "You like fucking with me, don't you? You like making me look bad! You wake up and say, 'Today I'm gonna fuck with Millweed!' and it makes you happy, doesn't it?"

And, we had no choice but to stand there and take it - hang our heads and blubber apologies and promise never to be hung over again, never to show up late again, because he held the ultimate trump card _ he could fire us and cut us off from the golden tit.

But once we were out on the course walking it off, the hanover and any cares associated with it (including Millweed) evaporated into the light mountain air.

And after the round, with our pockets replenished and our spirits restored by the carefree, self-congratulatory ebullience of the uberrich, we were powerless to resist the siren song of clinking glasses, the inviting golden light of the street lamps and tavern windows in town, and the slopeside hot tubs steaming under the stars.

We all jumped ship and dined, danced, and romanced the night away and then were dashed against the rocks of Millweed's wrath all over again the next morning."

-John Dunn, *Loopers: A Caddie's Twenty-Year Golf Odyssey*

"The Wolves are Coming" a sculpture on the 18th Hole, The Hills Golf Club, Arrowtown, New Zealand shows drama unfolding along the right side on the final fairway where there's an attack of 110 life-size cast-iron wolves against a sword wielding warrior

A final message to you from The Team at Golfwell: Above all, have fun in golf and enjoy all your adventures! Thank you for reading and best to you!

Read our other book: Absolutely Hilarious Adult Golf Joke Book at > www.amazon.com/Absolutely-Hilarious-Adult-Golf-Joke/dp/1530123542

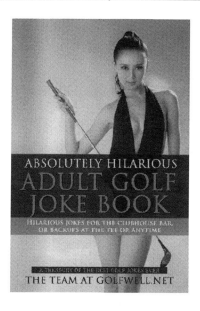

Thank you for taking an interest in our book. We hope you found it entertaining and had a few laughs.

If you enjoyed reading it, please consider leaving a review on Amazon so more readers can find this title.

We love questions or comments; so, don't be shy and feel free to contact us.

Thank you again.

The Team at Golfwell.net

info@Golfwell.net

Read more Golf Stories on our site at >> https://www.golfwell.net/golfwell-s-story-contest.html

Made in the USA
Lexington, KY
29 June 2018